The Conservative Tradition

EDITED BY

R. J. White

Fellow of Downing College
Cambridge

New York University Press

New York

First published in 1950

by Nicholas Kaye Ltd., London

First United States edition 1957

Manufactured in the United States of America

GENERAL PREFACE

ONE of the unique contributions the English people have made to civilisation has been the discussion of political issues which has been going on in Britain continuously since the sixteenth century. It is a discussion which has ranged over the whole field of political thought and experience. It began with the relation of the State to the individual in religious matters; for the last half century it has been increasingly preoccupied with the relation of the State to the individual in economic matters. The strength of tradition, the right of rebellion; the demand for equality, the rights of property; the place of justice and morality in foreign policy, the relations between Britain and her overseas territories; the claims of minorities, the value of civil and religious freedom; the rule of law, the Rule of the Saints; the rights of the individual, the claims of the State—all these have been the subject of passionate and incessant argument among Englishmen since the time of the Reformation.

This debate has never been of an academic character. There are, it is true, masterpieces of political philosophy in the English language: Hobbes' *Leviathan* is an obvious example. But the true character of this debate has been empirical: the discussion of particular and practical issues, in the course of which a clash of principle and attitude is brought out, but in which the element of abstract thought is always kept in relation to an immediate and actual situation. The riches of British political thought are to be found less in the philosophers' discussions of terms like 'The State', 'freedom' and 'obligation'—important though these are—than in the writings and speeches on contemporary political issues of men like Lilburne, Locke, Bolingbroke, Burke, Tom Paine, Fox, the Mills, Cobden, Disraeli, Gladstone, and the Fabians. No other literature in the world is so rich in political pamphlets as English, and the pages of *Hansard* are a mine not only for the historian of political events but also for the historian of political ideas. It is in the discussions provoked by the major crises in British history—the Civil War, the Revolt of the American Colonies, the Reform Bills of the nineteenth century—that our political ideas have been hammered out.

One unfortunate result of this is that much of the material which anyone interested in English political ideas needs to read is inaccessible. Pamphlets and speeches are often only to be found in contemporary publications hidden away on the more obscure shelves of the big libraries. Even when the reader has secured a volume of seventeenth-century pamphlets or of Gladstone's speeches, he may well be deterred by the large amount of now irrelevant detail or polemic through which he has to make his way before striking the characteristic ideas and assumptions of the writer or speaker. It is to meet the need of the reader who is interested in English political ideas but has neither the time, the patience, nor perhaps the opportunity, to read through a library of books to find the material he is looking for that this present series of books is designed. Its aim is to present from sources of the most varied kind, books, pamphlets, speeches, letters, newspapers, a selection of original material illustrating the different facets of Englishmen's discussion of politics. Each volume will include an introductory essay by the editor together with sufficient explanation of the circumstances to make each extract intelligible. In some cases it has seemed best to make a particular crisis the focus of the discussion: this has been done with Mr. Beloff's volume, 'The Debate on the American Revolution', and with Dr. Cobban's 'The Debate on the French Revolution'. In other cases the development of a particular view has been traced over a long period of years: this is the case for instance with the volumes on the Conservative, the Liberal, and the Radical Traditions. In a third case, that of the volume on 'Britain and Europe', our idea has been to single out a recurrent problem in English politics and trace its discussion from Pitt's day to our own.

To begin with, we have concentrated our attention on the period between the Revolt of the American Colonies and the Great War of 1914. When that has been covered we hope to treat the earlier period in the same way, notably the political discussions of the seventeenth century.

We do not believe that any one of these facets can be singled out and labelled as in some particular way more characteristic than others of the British Political Tradition: the rebels have as great a part in our political tradition as those who have argued the case for the claims of prescription and established authority. The wealth of that tradition is that it includes Lilburne, Tom Paine, Richard Cobden and the Early English Socialists as well as Locke, Burke and Disraeli.

We have tried to hold the balance even. In no sense do we wish to act as propagandists or advocates. While each editor has been given complete freedom to present his material as he wishes, we have been concerned as general editors to see that equal representation is given to different views in the series as a whole. Only in this way, we believe, is it possible to display the British Political Tradition in its unequalled richness, as built up out of a variety of political opinions and out of the clash between them, as the great and continuous debate of the nation to which, in its very nature, there can be no end.

ALAN BULLOCK

F. W. DEAKIN

Oxford

TABLE OF CONTENTS

ix

TABLE OF CONTENTS

xi

TABLE OF CONTENTS

B   xvii

Bull is a born Conservative; for this too I inexpressibly honour him. All great Peoples are Conservative. . . . CARLYLE

ACKNOWLEDGEMENT

The Editor acknowledges his grateful obligation to the following authors and publishers:

Lord Balfour, Messrs. Hodder and Stoughton, and A. P. Watt and Son, for permission to include a passage from the late Lord Balfour's *Opinions and Arguments.*

The Oxford University Press, for permission to quote from Lord Hugh Cecil's *Conservatism* (Home University Library).

Mr. T. S. Eliot and Messrs. Faber and Faber Ltd., for permission to quote certain passages from Mr. T. S. Eliot's *The Idea of a Christian Society.*

Mr. Quintin Hogg and Penguin Books Ltd., for permission to quote passages from *The Case for Conservatism.*

Lord Eustace Percy and Messrs. Heinemann Ltd., for permission to quote from an essay contributed by Lord Percy to *Conservatism and the Future* (1935).

Kenneth Pickthorn, Esq., for allowing quotation from his essay, *Principles and Prejudices* (Signpost Books, 1943).

The Earl of Portsmouth, and the Editor of *The Listener*, for permission to quote from two broadcast talks delivered by the Earl of Portsmouth in 1947.

Mr. G. M. Young, for permission to quote a passage from his essay, *Ourselves* (Signpost Books, 1944).

Grateful thanks are also due to the General Editors of the present series of volumes for much patient guidance and constructive criticism in the preparation of the text.

R. J. WHITE

Downing College
Cambridge
1950

INTRODUCTION

I

To put up Conservatism in a bottle with a label is like trying to liquefy the atmosphere or to give an accurate description of the beliefs of a member of the Anglican Church. The difficulty arises from the nature of the thing. For Conservatism is less a political doctrine than a habit of mind, a mode of feeling, a way of living. And the human content of the party is no less amorphous than the so-called "creed". The party is, in fact, the perfect secular analogy of its great historical ally, the Church of England. It contains not only the convinced and the converted who think they know what they believe. It contains also that vast residue of politics which would be hard put to it to describe itself as anything at all—the political equivalent of the millions who go down in the Army Records under "Religion" as "C. of E.". Snobs, idlers, millionaires, craftsmen, landladies, colour-sergeants, milliners, jockeys, innkeepers, academicians, men of genius as distinct from men of talent, anyone and everyone who thinks poetry, money-making, love and sport more important than politics: in fact, anyone with anything to lose, if it is only the opportunity to be idle—these are the Conservatives. It has also tended to be the party of the poor, as distinct from the working-class.

What holds this field full of folk together is obviously not so much a body of intellectually formulated principles as a number of instincts, and the governing instinct is the instinct of enjoyment. " Talk of ways of spreading a wholesome Conservatism throughout the country," Walter Bagehot once observed, " give painful lectures, distribute weary tracts . . . but as far as communicating and establishing your creed are concerned —try a little pleasure . . . So long as this world is this world, will a buoyant life be the proper source of an animated Conservatism." The political importance of this instinct of enjoyment, this largely thoughtless devotion to the life of here and now in all its richness and variety, is that it puts politics in its place as something secondary or incidental. The Conservative, or better still the Tory, may profess to subordinate politics to religion, to the attainment of the Beatific Vision. When he thinks about it at all, he would no doubt say that that is what it comes to. But immediately, when he is not thinking about it, he subordinates politics to the enjoyably strenuous activities of daily living. This fact makes him peculiarly susceptible to the charms of politicians who promise to leave him alone. It has meant that he has been led by the nose for long periods by crooks and charlatans. But it also means that when he does formulate his politics they have a profound depth of reference to the real life of men in society. The shape and pattern of Conservative politics have rarely been imposed upon the phenomena of nature, and of human nature, by clever men taking thought. In so far as Conservatism is a formulated doctrine, it is the by-product of real living, not the fabrication of unimpeded intellect. It has arisen out of nature, out of human nature, like the great, spare, necessary lines of a landscape seen in the perspective of history: the stuff of life disciplined by its own inherent necessities rather than by the fiat of a lawgiver.

To discover the order which inheres in things rather than to impose an order upon them; to strengthen and perpetuate that order rather than to dispose things anew according to some formula which may be nothing more than a fashion; to legislate along the grain of human nature rather than against it; to pursue limited objectives with a watchful eye; to amend here, to prune there; in short, to preserve the method of nature in the conduct of the state—because nature, as Burke observed, is wisdom without reflection and above it: this is Conservatism. Its method is Aristotelian, its temper sceptical. It has none of the dogmatic fervour of Continental parties of the "Right." It abhors the use of force as a political weapon by majorities and minorities alike: salutary experience as a proscribed minority taught English Toryism the value of the rule of law and the futility of *coups d'état* in the hard school of Jacobitism in the eighteenth century. It takes men as they are, children of nature under Divine Providence, finite beings, prone to error, capable of becoming something decent with discipline, but more than likely to become something less than men without it. While concerning itself with improvement, it never forgets that a very considerable part of human effort and energy must always be expended in preventing things from getting worse. To say that the Conservative is distinguished by a profound attachment to the theory of Original Sin would be an over-simplification. It is enough to say that he sees that a theory of progress is a delusion unless it is accompanied by a proper awareness of the ever-present forces of degeneration which afflict man's imperfect will.

Once you have accepted man for what he is, once you have replaced perfectionism by improvement, once you have learned to postpone the Kingdom of God to the timeless plane of the *Civitas Dei*, then the principles of Conservatism become clear. They are three in number. The first is the radical inadequacy of the political as a final account of man; the second is the organic conception of society; the third is the rejection of " Will " as the sanction, or sanctification, of law. All Conservative political thinking, and all Conservative policies, spring from these original concepts.

First, the inadequacy of politics. Conservatism sees men not under a political but under a cosmological order. Politics is therefore a means to an end beyond politics. It is not that the Conservative is more religious than other men, but that he is less confident than some other men about man's self-dependence, more inclined to mistrust the finality of man-made remedies for human ills, more prone to look for the source of these ills rather in a defective human nature than in defective laws and institutions. This peculiar scepticism about political or economic remedies for all the ills of human flesh, is at its best re-inforced by an attachment to the moral free-agency of the individual. You *can* make men moral by Act of Parliament, but to what purpose if the operation of the law is merely external to the individual? Unless our actions are the result (the " language ", Coleridge called it) of the moral state of the agent, our virtues will be like wax fruit tied on to the sprays of a fruit tree by the hand of prudence. This is the highest ground upon which Conservatives resist the intrusion of state-power into certain spheres of the citizen's life. Conservatism champions that diminishing thing, " the private life ", not as a form of escapism but as a sphere of moral free-agency. For man is himself finally responsible to his Maker for himself,

4

and he is so because he has a Maker. Once he gets rid of the idea of his dependence upon something, or some one, beyond himself—in fact, upon God—he will never rest until he has found a substitute to remedy his ineluctable sense of his own insufficiency. The nearest thing to hand is that mortal God, the State. But once you believe in God, it has been remarked, you thereby acquire the right to question everything else. The political scepticism of the Conservative springs from his sense of religion, and is the source of his freedom.

Conservatism is not, and has never been, a " High State Theory ". High-state idealism, that dissolute doctrine which from Rousseau and Hegel down to Bernard Bosanquet would identify liberty with obedience to the law, is a suitable doctrine for Jacobins, Junkers and National Socialists, but it is a poison which English Conservatism has always rejected with the anti-toxic strength of its own essentially protestant theory of Christian liberty. The laws of the state, says the Conservative, are made by men, and like men they are imperfect. Obedience to the laws is nearly always right; certainly the upholding of the laws is the first defence of liberty. But there is nothing sacred about the laws. The palladium of English liberty is not the laws themselves (which have often been bad), but the rule of law—the steady enforcement of a few precious principles which have been found by the strictest tests of practice over many centuries best to serve the ends of human personality. These few principles, and the wholly utilitarian devices which Englishmen have evolved for their maintenance and enforcement—of which the most precious are freedom from arbitrary arrest and imprisonment, and the right to public trial by a jury of one's fellow citizens under the direction of

5

independent judges—these rights of Englishmen at law have gone abroad and blossomed under the generalising passions of less empirical peoples into universal " Rights of Man ". The English have never cared for this, their novel and high-falutin cut and fashion. They still call them " the rights of Englishmen ", and they know (or they knew until lately) how and where to enforce them in their concrete reality.

Conservatism has been the ceaseless champion of this concrete conception of the Englishman's rights at common law, the remorseless critic of its perversion into philosophical " Rights of Man at Nature ". It was the Conservative Burke, not the Radical Bentham, who disposed of Natural Rights of Man as a relevant political concept. Bentham, with his " nonsense on stilts ", was little more than abusive. Burke showed that the only real rights of man are his rights at law within civil society, and that to measure them up against abstract " Rights at Nature " is to attempt to institute a comparison between the incomparable. " Men cannot enjoy the rights of an uncivil and of a civil state together." The Burkian, historical, concrete conception of rights needs to be emphasised more than ever to-day, as the classic Conservative doctrine, because a fashion has grown up in some quarters of identifying Conservative teaching on this matter with the teaching of the so-called " Natural Law " school—most respectably represented in the modern world by the Roman Catholic Church. The trouble with Natural Law is, and always has been, that it gets a variable content according to whatever authority happens to be teaching it. Unless the concept is to be unbearably woolly, it is necessary to accept a content laid down by an authoritarian church, or—what is worse—a body of Professors, claiming to speak in the name of what is called "the right reason of mankind". Conservatives would do better to stick to Burke.[1]

The mistaken attribution of a High-state theory to Conservatism has largely arisen from the fact that Conservatism has always upheld an organic theory of society. When that great lover of liberty, that profound champion of individual moral responsibility, Samuel Taylor Coleridge, met Harriet Martineau he is said to have observed: "You seem to look on society as an aggregate of individuals," and the great lady-Liberal replied promptly: "Of course I do." Now, to the Tory, or the Conservative, that blithe assurance is incredible. To him, the ultimate individuality of the individual it not a political but a religious concept. To him, it is only the church that is concerned with men as individuals. "A State", Coleridge observed, "regards classes, and not individuals; and it estimates classes, not by internal merit, but external accidents, as property, birth, etc. But a Church does the reverse of this, and disregards all external accidents, and looks at men as individual persons, allowing no gradations of rank. but such as greater or less wisdom, learning and holiness ought to confer. A Church is, therefore, in idea, the only pure democracy." For the State to regard individual persons as the ultimate elements in society, and to attempt to operate directly upon a universalised individuality, is for the State to arrogate to itself the claims and functions of a Church. This is precisely what the State has attempted to do in those disastrous epochs when politics have become the agent of an

[1] See *The Case for Conservatism* by Quintin Hogg, Chapter 12, and an essay in criticism by Michael Oakeshott, "Contemporary British Politics", in the *Cambridge Journal*, May 1948 (Vol. I, No. 8).

ideology: in the Puritan Revolution of the seventeenth century, in the Jacobin phase of the French Revolution, and in the Fascist and Communist Revolutions of the twentieth century. The root of all tyranny is the assumption of a quasi-religious function by state-power, or the usurpation of the whole field of human activity and experience by politics. Conservatism rejects this assumption, this usurpation, without compromise, and the source of its strength in so doing is to be discovered in its initial insistence that society is not a collection of " universalised individuals ", nor the sum of individuals statistically aggregated, but the product of a system of real relationships *between* individuals, classes, groups and interests.

This conception of society as a complex of real relationships rather than a sum of individuals, is the product of historical fact and empirical observation. The Conservative would be the last to deny that groups, families, crafts, religious congregations, " interests ", corporations of all kinds, have often been inimical in their activities to the general good. But he holds that to destroy them is to throw out the baby with the bath-water. He holds that it is one of the functions of state-power to regulate their activities, to adjust their conflicts, to protect persons and property against their excessive busy-ness. But he would at the same time cherish their well-regulated life in the interest both of social vitality and an ordered liberty. Hobbes called them weakening worms in the entrails of Leviathan. Rousseau would prohibit them in the interest of " the general will ". Burke bade us love " the little platoon ", the subdivision, as the nursery of civic virtue and larger affections. Without the creative principle of voluntary action and a healthy degree of self-organisation the organic life of society perishes in the arms of an efficient despotism, even though it takes unto itself the sacred name of democracy. The purpose of government is not to concentrate but to diffuse power. Diffusion of power is the characteristic of organic life, just as concentration of power is the characteristic of mechanism. It is in a dynamo, not in a tree, that power is to be found at a single point, source or centre. And a dynamo can be put out of action by a single blow of a hammer, while a tree dies by inches. Even in terms of mere survival-value, it were better that a state should be a tree than an engine.

Finally, Conservatism rejects the concept of will as the sanction of law. " If government were a matter of will upon any side," Burke told his constituents at Bristol, in 1774, " yours, without question, ought to be superior. But government and legislation are matters of reason and judgement, and not inclination." That is not only the traditional Conservative conception of the nature of government and legislation; it is the traditional English conception. The notion that law is given its validity by the mere will of its maker, whether it be the will of a Prince or of a popularly elected assembly, lacks all reputable ancestry in the English, or the Conservative, tradition of morals and politics. The idea that law is what the people's representatives have been given a mandate to make it, appeared briefly during the Cromwellian period. It has appeared again in the politics of Socialism. Its affinities with the Bonapartist (and Hitlerite) politics of the plebiscite are too obvious to need emphasis. Conservatism rejects it without compromise as inimical to freedom and morality.

If law is not validated by the will of the Prince, or

a majority of the People, or any other political entity, by what is it validated? To answer, as some have done, that is based on, or must be consonant with, " Reason ", is simply to raise the further question — " Whose reason? " To go further and equate what is reasonable with what is " natural ", in the sense of conforming with a concept of " natural law ", still leaves the question unanswered—who, or what, is the judge of what is " natural "? Conservatives would prefer to say (as Marxists say of any embarrassing question) that the original question is one that ought not to be asked; but they say it not because they fear they might get an embarrassing answer, but because it has no practical political bearings. Government being an empirical art, and having nothing to do with ideology, it is not concerned with the conformity of law to will, reason, or nature, except in the purely expediential sense that it is obvious that law must have some relation to popular feeling, to the observed behaviour, customs and manners of a given people; that it plainly must not contravene common sense; and that it will not be obeyed if it outrages the elementary laws of nature. No one in his senses will make laws that are irksome to the people without a pretty shrewd notion that the people expect, or wish, or can be persuaded to expect and wish, to suffer irksome restraint for the sake of some obviously greater benefit. Nor is anyone going to make laws requiring everyone to wear a number fifteen collar, or requiring that water shall in future flow uphill of its own accord.

II

Conservatism was, to all intents and purposes, invented by Sir Robert Peel in the decade which followed the passing of the Great Reform Bill. Its purpose, as elaborated by Peel in the Tamworth Manifesto, was to defend on strictly utilitarian grounds the traditional institutions of the country in Church and State, to promote the reform of proved abuses, and to resist the restless spirit of innovation: in fact, to combine the Burke of the *Reflections* with the Burke of the Economical Reform Bill. The governing idea of Conservatism at its birth was thus " Continuity ". Quite literally, it was to conserve in the light of a rational reading of traditional institutions. Its negative motto might have been Burke's aphorism that a passion for innovation is the character of small minds; its positive precept his opinion that " early reformations are amicable arrangements with a friend in power; late reformations are terms imposed upon a conquered enemy . . ."

Now the Conservative Tradition means a great deal more than this, and it is only by reference to the history of the Party that it is possible to reveal all that it means. The idea of continuity, of conservation in the name of continuity, of the superiority of evolution over revolution, were the natural and necessary things to stress in the age of Burke and Peel. It was dialectically necessary, as well as fortunate, that the Jacobin contempt for history should beget its opposite, even if it was not necessary for it to beget the ancestor-worship of Burke. The emergence of Conservatism might equally well be historically justified by the indispensability of a *vis inertiae* in any system of political dynamics, and Peel himself could enumerate simple resistance to change as one of the legitimate and fruitful functions of Conservatisms in all situations and at all times. But if this were all that Conservatism means, it would long since have perished of equivocation and redundancy. Too much talk about conservation has always an equivocal sound in the mouths of rich men. Moreover, the idea of continuity is no monopoly of Conservatism. All English parties, from left to right (with the exception of the Communist Party, which anyway is not English), claim to defend the English Constitution, the traditional institutions of England, or the "English way of life." Conservatism as "continuity" is not enough.

Conservatism was a natural child of the age of the French Revolution; its parents were Burke and Peel; and for a time it seemed likely to grow up a Whig. There was a great deal of Whiggery, repentant or potential, about both its parents. What saved it was the wondrous imagination of a Jewish stepfather, who made the growing boy understand that he was heir to something much older than fear of the French Revolution, that grandfather Burke's Whiggery was his least desirable feature, and that father Peel didn't know what he was talking about. Disraeli was irreverent but right. The old "Whig trumpeter", Mr. Burke, had the root of the matter in him; beneath his Whiggery there was a real grasp of the nature and purposes of society. And Sir Robert Peel, for all his honest adaptation of means to ends, really did not know what those ends were—what society really is, and how it lives in its organic vitality (though, it is true, he did once express a doubt about the desirability of our becoming a spinning-jenny kind of nation). Disraeli did know these things. He knew that there was a Tory tradition which answered to the nature of men in both their immediate and their ultimate purposes, the tradition of an organic as distinct from an artificial society, and he brought this great tradition into Conservatism as a constructive force for the furtherance of positive purposes. Continuity, conservation, resistance, all such defensive and largely negative concepts, were to be transcended by a concrete realisation of the inherent principles by which society lives and moves and has its being. Burke had known it; it was all to be found in the *Reflections*, although men had read it for its Whiggish " panic of property " rather than for its positive teaching on the true nature of political societies. Coleridge had known it, too, and Carlyle; but the one had spoken from the clouds of philosophy, and the other had gone off to look for stainless moral heroes. Disraeli was neither a philosopher nor a moralist. His inspiration was history. To him, Toryism was the political expression of the traditional English society. He injected its concepts into Conservatism, and they are there still, its justification and its inspiration.

The concepts which give to Conservatism its positive character are the alluvial deposit of a society which has passed away. We may, if we wish to use labels, call that society feudal. It was certainly aristocratic, and it was generally Christian. Its principal political characteristic was a reflection of its cosmology: the principle of hierarchy, or degree. With this went the conception of power and authority as a trust: the mutual obligation of every man, and every order, from the King downwards. Power being a trust, the co-efficient of power in the form of material—or property —was likewise a trust. The burden of authority was thought to be rightfully accompanied by the enjoyment of honour; and, for perfectly sound utilitarian reasons, those who governed and fought and prayed had to be maintained by those who didn't. " Honours ",

" Liberties ", " Franchises ", great and small, were not merely the rewards but the material and honourable bases of political, judicial and ecclesiastical functions. To hold one's place within this vast hierarchy, to be " worshipful " according to one's degree, and to perform and receive one's obligations to those above and below oneself : this was to live according to the universal frame of things—according to the laws of God and Nature. Not to be " tied to the soil ", to become a " landless man ", in some sort, was not " emancipation " but horror. The ideal was not freedom in the sense of getting loose from obligations. The ideal was status—to have a standing, a place, a " liberty ", one's own peculiar form of privilege. For originally all liberties were privileges, all rights were the concomitant of duties.

It is easy to see how deeply Toryism is coloured by the historical experience of the feudal and Christian centuries. Europe was made, said Burke, by Christianity and the spirit of a gentleman, and he proceeded, in his great onslaught upon the Jacobin political geometers, to formulate from the facts, the values, and even the fictions, of the traditional society of western Europe, that body of ideas that we now know as the political philosophy of Conservatism: the organic and hierarchical nature of society, the differentiation of functions within that society, and the consequent political inequality of men, together with the diffusion of entrusted power as the essential safeguard of freedom. This same great vision of the values of an older Europe was seen through the mists of poppy and mandragora by S. T. Coleridge. Further removed from the Revolution than Burke, and more deeply read in the history of the sixteenth and seventeenth centuries,

Coleridge was able to see the Revolution in the dialectic of history, and when he looked back beyond the Jacobins it was not to the *ancien régime* of Marie Antoinette or to the supposed ages of faith and chivalry, but to the Platonic tradition of Sidney, Shakespeare and Milton, and to the Protestant libertarianism of the centuries since the Renaissance. He brought to Conservatism a philosophic emphasis upon the moral free-agency of the individual within an organic society, which served to correct the incipient state-worship of Burke, and a dialectical treatment of history which could afford a legitimate theory of progress emancipated from ancestor-worship. Coleridge's position within the Conservative tradition is secure, but it is too little understood even by Conservatives — which is probably the fault of his tangential style rather than of their reluctance to learn from him.[1]

After the Irishman and the Englishman came the inspired Jew. Putting aside Disraeli's gorgeous nonsense —and there was a wonderful lot of it—he did more than any other single mind to make modern Conservatism an intellectual synthesis capable of influencing a society which had outlived the conditions which gave it birth. When Disraeli wrote and spoke his best thoughts, the society which lived according to the organic, hierarchical ideas of Burke and Coleridge had given place to the rootless, irresponsibly individualistic society of the industrial revolution. Disraeli's analysis, in his novels, of this jungle-society, with its class-warfare, its " intolerable serfage ", and its mutually ignorant

---

[1] *Vide* Lord Liverpool's endorsement of a letter from Coleridge in 1817: " From Mr Coleridge, stating that the object of his writings has been to rescue speculative philosophy from false principles of reasoning . . . at least, I believe this is Mr Coleridge's meaning, but I cannot well understand him."

nations, and his castigation of the liberal-bourgeois complacency about free contract, free competition and economic free-booting in general, were as trenchant as those of Carlyle, and aroused the enthusiasm even of Marx.[1] His remedies, when they took the form of cracking up feudalism (chiefly, one imagines, in order to annoy Mr Cobden and Mr Bright), or an appeal for leadership by an enlightened *noblesse* full of *oblige* towards a grateful and loyal working-class, and full of aristocratic scorn for a vulgar bourgeoisie which was the enemy of both, could scarcely command serious attention in a society whose aristocracy was chiefly concerned with mortgages and partridges, and whose working class was chiefly concerned to climb into the middle class. If he had gone no further than this, Disraeli would now be remembered as a rather disingenuous ally of noble young sentimentalists like George Smythe and Lord John Manners.

Disraeli, however, like Burke, was not only a political thinker but a party politician. It was his business to apply and adapt traditional principles within the imperatives of an ever-changing social and political environment. He combined Burke's imaginative grasp of ideas with Peel's mighty sense of the necessary and the possible, and the combination was decisive. Peel had found the Tory Party encumbered in its appeal to an increasingly industrial and urban community by the odium which, for all the liberalism of Liverpool and Canning, must have accrued to any government trying to govern England between Waterloo and Peterloo. Although the Party upheld the Corn Laws and opposed the Great Reform Bill on respectable principles sincerely held, its reasons were not persuasive

[1] Communist Manifesto.

16

to the manufacturers, shop-keepers and superior artisans whose suffrages were to rule Victorian England. Peel invented the " Conservative " Party to win some share of the favour of these rising interests, and, although he broke it over the Corn Laws, his work was not in vain. Disraeli made his somewhat equivocal reputation by his onslaught upon the " organised hypocrisy " of Conservatism in the name of a traditional Toryism, but the Party that he came to lead was made possible by the work of Peel. It was Peel who organised the post-1832 electorate and rallied the middle-classes behind a programme of loyalty to the revised Constitution, of adherence to the ancient institutions of Church and State, and of timely reform of proved abuses. It was the indispensable basis for any kind of Conservatism that was to survive, let alone triumph, in the new era.

" A sound Conservative government? " Disraeli mocked. " I understand: Tory men and Whig measures." He was right. It was time to call a halt to a Conservatism which preached loyalty to ancient institutions so long as they did not govern and played into the hands of a capitalist class without responsibilities. It was not enough to bewail bitterly the contrast of past and present, of feudal responsibility and the bastard feudalism of the mills, of monastic charity and the Bastilles of the New Poor Law. Feudalism and monasticism were dead. Lordship and kingship survived in pageantry but not in power. The territorial constitution with its spirit of " vicinage " was giving place to the administrative centralisation of Whitehall. The gentlemen of the parish were being supplanted by salaried state-servants. The organic and aristocratic society simply could not survive the impact of the steam-engine. But the values of the older society could, and must, survive. That is what Disraeli saw and never ceased to say. All the best minds of the age—Carlyle, Ruskin, Matthew Arnold—saw and said it. It is what distinguishes Disraeli alone among the working politicians and party leaders and national statesmen of the nineteenth century.

The Party had now, for the first time, a leader who saw, and said, and believed, that society must get itself " organic filaments " or perish in despotism and slavery; that the " two nations " in their mutual ignorance and hatred must become one nation by a revived sense of the responsibilities of property on the one hand, and a revived (and legally guaranteed) sense of the status of labour on the other; that the sources of refreshment and vitality of a nation's life are to be found not at Whitehall but in the municipality, the parish, the congregation, the university, the school, the family; that men are worshipful and worshipping creatures, equal before God and the laws, but unequal in all else; that hierarchy is of the order of nature and privilege the reward of honourable service. Burke had said that these things were; Coleridge had rather despondently said that they still should be; Disraeli, with the power of a legislator, tried to make them so. It was twenty years too late, he said, when he became Prime Minister in 1874; he had been in politics for more than forty years, and had but seven years to live. The legislation of his Ministry was little more than an earnest of his beliefs and intentions. The codification and extension of the Factory Acts and the Enclosure Act of 1876 re-inforced the responsibilities of capital; two Trade Union Acts did more for the legal status of labour than any other legislation in the century; the

Public Health Act and the Artisans' Dwelling Act encouraged the social responsibilities of the municipalities. His cult of the Queen, together with his personal, if somewhat unconvincing, devotion to the Established Church as a teaching body that should speak with one voice and uphold a dogmatic creed, are the best instances of his insistence upon the reality of the national institutions.

By his recall of Conservatism to the great heritage of Toryism, Disraeli taught Conservatives to put their faith in two things: the historic institutions of the nation, and " the invigorating energies of an educated and enfranchised people." These compose the final synthesis of Tory Democracy. The national institutions embody this Toryism, since they are the symbols of, the political pattern produced by, and safeguarding, the organic life of the nation. The invigorating energies of an educated and enfranchised people are the guarantee of democracy. Peel had turned Conservatism from the preserve of a frightened landed interest into the national party concerned with the well-being of the whole community. Disraeli gave the national claims of the party a philosophy and a programme. It was his boast that he had lived to see the end of the Liberal monopoly of reformism, that he had equated Conservatism with, if not the popular will, then with the popular interest. Whatever may be said of the immediate motives and tactics that produced the Reform Act of 1867, Disraeli had been true to his ideals. He had said, at the time of the repeal of the Corn Laws, that if the preponderance of the landed interest were to be replaced by the irresponsible tyranny of industrial capitalism, it would be necessary to call in the mass of the people to restore the balance.

" Instead of falling under . . . the thraldom of capital—under those who, while they boast of their intelligence, are more proud of their wealth—if we must find a new force to maintain the ancient throne and monarchy of England, I, for one, hope that we may find that novel power in the invigorating energies of an educated and enfranchised people." That is the key-phrase in the history of Tory Democracy. It meant that the numerical nation must be brought to direct participation in the political life of the country in order to preserve what the landed community could no longer preserve—the institutions, and therefore the liberties, of England. The policy of Peel, he protested—with less than justice to that great patriot's intentions—had delivered England into the hands of the worst of all oligarchies—the oligarchy of a middle-class Liberalism that was illiberal because it was not truly popular, an oligarchy of business that was unnational because it was undisciplined by those traditions of service, obligation and charity which had tempered the rule of a landed aristocracy. To call in the people would be to call in the nation.

That the Conservative Party alone could, and should, rally the mass of the people in defence of the national institutions, and thereby defeat the sectionalism of a professedly " liberal " or a class-conscious " labour " party, depended upon Conservatism identifying itself with the interests of every section of the community. It did not happen. Disraeli produced the Conservative working-man, but there were not enough of him. The leadership of the Party fell to Salisbury and Balfour, statesmen possessed of every moral and intellectual virtue save those of energy and imagination. The one man after Disraeli who seemed for a time to have something of the stature of the master was Lord Randolph Churchill, and his career was cut short by his own intransigence after a brief spasm of sharp-shooting under the big guns of Hatfield. Churchill was always something of a political jackanapes. He hugged the mantle of Elisha round his elegant and rather sloping shoulders with the air of a pocket swashbuckler and all the cheek of a fifth-former trying it on with the Headmaster. But, at any rate, Lord Randolph saw what was happening, and what was going to happen, if the magisterial somnolence of the very rich and the very rare neglected, or thwarted, the realities of a democratic Toryism. Like Peel, at another remove, he fought for the re-organisation of the Party on more democratic lines, and he gave due warning that unless Conservatism could rally the masses of labour to the cause of the national institutions, Labour would use those institutions for its sectional interests as the landed aristocracy and the industrial oligarchy in their turn had done, and that the process might result in their being swept away. This was uncomfortable prognostication, and a great sigh of relief went up from Hatfield when the end came in 1886.[1]

The year 1886—five years after the death of Disraeli —was the turning-point in the history of modern Conservatism. It was not only the year of the fall of Randolph Churchill. It was the year of the great Liberal schism over Gladstone's Home Rule policy. Henceforth the Conservative ranks were to be swollen by the injured or apprehensive propertied interests in flight from the radicalism of the " old man in a hurry." The party which had broken Peel with " the best brute

---

[1] Churchill resigned from Salisbury's Cabinet on Dec. 22nd, 1886. He died in 1895.

votes in England " was to grow once more into the great bulwark of " vested interests " which could win everything—even the South African War—except the hearts and imaginations of honest men. Sometimes it was a case of its left hand not knowing what its right hand was doing, as when the *ci-devant* Radical, Joseph Chamberlain, sincerely tried to persuade the working classes that preferential tariffs for the greater unity of the Empire were also the answer to unemployment. Sometimes the left hand simply gave in to the right hand, as when the liberal Balfour gave in to the mineowners of the Rand over the importation of indentured Chinese labour into the Transvaal. At all times, the high Imperial idealism of Beaconsfield was likely to slide into a shoddy cult of " the imperial mission of the Anglo-Saxon race." There were fine things, too, like the work of Sir Robert Morant for education, but they were too few, or they were purchased at too high a price in terms of compromise with interests which it was the duty of a truly traditional Toryism not to placate but to subdue. By 1906 the game was up. In the twilight of the gods which supervened, sundry strange figures from Bewdley and Birmingham were to be seen smoking pipes and fishing trout-streams.

III

It is an unsafe partition, Coleridge once observed, that divides opinions without principle from unprincipled opinions. Conservatism has always survived the worst consequences of its own weaknesses of inattention and complacency. Nor is there anything remarkable or novel in parties becoming identified with " interests "—sinister or otherwise. " As long as the connection subsists between man's reason and his self-love," wrote James Madison, nearly two centuries ago, "his opinions and his passions will have a reciprocal influence on each other; and the former will be objects to which the latter attach themselves." Because parties, like churches, are prone to error, because men are always falling below their best selves, because their reason never remains uncontaminated for long by their self-love, parties are forever in need of refreshment at the springs of doctrine. The passages that follow have been put together not without a hope that Conservatives may know what they believe, and act upon what they know. They are not intended to supply the documentary history of the Conservative Party, but a documentary exposition of the finest tradition in English political thinking, the tradition to which Conservatism must constantly refer if it is to maintain its validity in face of the problems of our time. The exposition ends, for reasons connected with the scope and purpose of this series of volumes, with the "Chamberlain Tradition" as represented by the great Joseph. When Joseph Chamberlain died, the greatest leader of the party in the present century was a leading light among the Liberals: that is the only reason why he is not represented here. Similar considerations account for the exclusion of such welcome signs of the revival of the great tradition as are to be found in Anthony Eden's exposition of the ideal of a "property-owning democracy" and restoration of the worker's status in industry. Signs of the times are all about us, and there is no way into the future—least of all for Conservatives—that does not stem from the ways opened for us by our fathers. Burke may fittingly have the last word, as he has the first: "People will not look forward to posterity who never look backward to their ancestors. . . . All the reformations we have hitherto made have proceeded upon the principle of reference to antiquity; and I hope, nay I am persuaded, that all those which possibly may be made hereafter, will be carefully formed upon analogical precedent, authority and example."

Part I

THE TRADITION

A Tory is one who, believing that the institutions of this country are calculated, as they were intended, to secure the prosperity and happiness of every class of society, wishes to maintain them in their original beauty, simplicity and integrity. He is tenacious of the rights of all, but most of the poor and needy, because they require the shelter of the constitution and the laws more than the other classes. A Tory is the staunch friend of Order for the sake of Liberty; and knowing that all our institutions are founded upon Christianity, he is of course a Christian, believing with St. Paul that each order of society is mutually dependent on the others for peace and prosperity, and that, although there " are many members, yet there is but one body. And the eye cannot say unto the hand, I have no need of you. Nay much more, those members of the body which seem to be more feeble are necessary." Sir, I am just such a Tory; or if you prefer it in my own words, as I once defined it to the Duke of Wellington when he asked " What do you mean by Toryism? " you shall have it: I replied, " My Lord Duke I mean a place for everything, and everything in its place."

RICHARD OASTLER

I am, and my father was before me, a violent Tory of the old school; (Walter Scott's school, that is to say, and Homer's). I name these two out of the numberless great Tory writers, because they were my own two masters . . . From my own chosen masters, then, Scott and Homer, I learned the Toryism which my best after-thought has only served to confirm. That is to say, a most sincere love of Kings, and dislike of everybody who attempted to disobey them. Only, both by Homer and Scott, I was taught strange ideas about Kings, which I find for the present much obsolete; for, I perceived that both the author of the Iliad and the author of Waverley made their Kings, or king-loving persons, do harder work than anybody else . . . I observed that they not only did more, but in proportion to their doings, *got* less than other people. . . .

JOHN RUSKIN

By the Conservative cause I mean the splendour of the Crown, the lustre of the Peerage, the privileges of the Commons, the rights of the poor. I mean that harmonious union, that magnificent concord of all interests, of all classes, on which our national greatness depends.

BENJAMIN DISRAELI

CHAPTER I

HUMAN NATURE AND POLITICS

This section begins with religious aphorisms; it goes on to illustrate the views of Conservative thinkers on man's "mixed and sensitive nature"; from this follows the Conservative view of the secondary importance of politics; finally, it illustrates the Conservative view of the art of politics, or statesmanship, which must follow from these premises—namely, that it is essentially an empirical science.

(i) *Aphorisms on the Religious Basis of Civil Society*

We know, and it is our pride to know, that man is by his constitution a religious animal . . . We know, and what is better, we inwardly feel, that religion is the basis of civil society, and the source of all good, and of all comfort.

EDMUND BURKE

Religion, true or false, is and ever has been the centre of gravity in a realm, to which all other things must and will accommodate themselves.

S. T. COLERIDGE

The most powerful principle which governs man is the religious principle. . . . Man was made to adore and to obey.

BENJAMIN DISRAELI

If Conservatives do not believe politics to be the most important thing in life, the great majority of them believe man to be a religious animal even before he is a political animal; it is precisely for this reason that they deny to politics, to the organised force of the State, the right to act upon the religious plane, to pursue ideal aims. . . .

KENNETH PICKTHORN

There can be no genuine Conservatism which is not founded upon a religious view of the basis of civil obligation, and there can be no true religion where the basis of civil obligation is treated as purely secular.

QUINTIN HOGG

(ii) *The Complexity of Human Nature: Reason and Prejudice*

The following passage is taken from Burke's *Reflections on the Revolution in France* (1790), the greatest onslaught upon purely rationalistic politics ever written. The need to insist upon the complexity of man's nature shows itself principally at times of crisis, because it is at those times that Radical political creeds— Jacobin, Utilitarian, Marxist, etc. — come forward with some simplified version of human nature in the interest of "social engineering" or "political geometry". Burke was face to face with the Jacobin simplification of man. He did little more than dogmatically assert its opposite.

The nature of man is intricate; the objects of society are of the greatest possible complexity: and therefore no simple disposition or direction of power can be suitable either to man's nature, or to the quality of his affairs. When I hear the simplicity of contrivance aimed at and boasted of in any new political constitutions, I am at a loss to decide that the artificers are grossly ignorant of their trade, or totally negligent of their duty. The simple governments are fundamentally defective, to say no worse of them. . . .

We are afraid to put men to live and trade each on his own private stock of reason; because we suspect that the stock in each man is small, and that the individuals would do better to avail themselves of the general bank and capital of nations and of ages. Many of our men of speculation, instead of exploding general prejudices, employ their sagacity to discover the latent wisdom which prevails in them. If they find what they seek, and they seldom fail, they think it more wise to continue the prejudice, with the reason involved, than to cast away the coat of prejudice, and to leave nothing but the naked reason; because prejudice, with its reason, has a motive to give action to that reason, and an affection which will give it permanence. Prejudice is of ready application in the emergency; it previously engages the mind in a steady course of wisdom and virtue, and does not leave the man hesitating in the moment of decision, sceptical, puzzled, and unresolved. Prejudice renders a man's virtue his habit; and not a series of unconnected acts. Through just prejudice, his duty becomes part of his nature.

(iii) *The Secondary Importance of Politics*

Because Conservatives believe that man is a religious animal and a creature of infinite complexity, they are sceptical about the ultimate claims of politics upon men's enthusiasm or interests. They distrust simple-minded faith in political contrivances or mechanism. Most of all, they condemn all attempts to set up the Kingdom of God on earth by a doctrine backed by force. It is typical of the Conservative attitude that Kenneth Pickthorn heads the first section of his essay, *Principles and Prejudices* (Signpost Books, 1943), with the words "How and why politics matter". The following passages are taken from that essay.

Politics do not really matter quite so much as is generally assumed in public discussion: for the talking and writing about them are done mostly by those who have a finger in politics or an itch for politics, and it is not new for cobblers and botchers to assume that there is nothing like leather. To most men, probably to still more women, immediate personal relations, for instance, matter much more than politics. To everyone who believes that there are any eternal values, any realities beyond this world and this life, clearly those eternities must matter immensely more than the politics of a day or even of a century. . . . This . . . is one of the reasons (though there are others of which Conservatives should be ashamed) why Conservatives are comparatively lukewarm, why they get up steam more intermittently, and why of the steam which they do get up they use a smaller proportion for pushing the party engine. . . .

Conservatives . . . are wise not to be too quickly or too wholly interested in politics, not to put all their eggs in that basket. . . . The Progressive believes fixedly that the fads of the contemporary mind at its best (especially his own) are a way to absolute good; and the Communist knows certainly that what he learns from Marx is dialectically necessary and materially determined; thus both are apt to put their own motives on the highest plane they can conceive, and therefore to authorise themselves to use force upon the motives of others. In other words, they are apt to assume that the State (when they control it) can and may (and therefore must) act directly on the spiritual and moral plane; that it has not merely the right to direct the conduct of each of its subjects in the interests of all, but also the duty to control their motives towards its conception of the universe. The oldest and most harmful of all forms of materialism is the attempt to set up the Kingdom of God by force. The attempt is none the better because God is called Dialectical Materialism or Racial Destiny or Modern Progress (or the New Order or the Common Man).

(iv) *Fox-hunting and Fun First*

Mr. Quintin Hogg's book, *The Case for Conservatism* (Penguin Books, 1947), opens, in traditionally Conservative fashion, with an attempt to delimit the sphere and scope of politics. It is perhaps the best, and certainly the most vigorous, expression of the attitude by a living writer.

Conservatives do not believe that political struggle is the most important thing in life. In this they differ from Communists, Socialists, Nazis, Fascists, Social Creditors and most members of the British Labour Party. The simplest among them prefer fox-hunting—the wisest religion. To the great majority of Conservatives, religion, art, study, family, country, friends, music, fun, duty, all the joy and riches of existence of which the poor no less than the rich are the indefeasible free-holders, all these are higher in the scale than their hand-maiden, the political struggle. This makes them easy to defeat—at first. . . . It will win in the end. Whatever the fanatics may think, in this at least Conservatives have the vast majority on their side. The man who puts politics first is not fit to be called a civilised being, let alone a Christian. . . .

The Conservative does not believe that the power of politics to put things right in this world is unlimited. This is partly because there are inherent limitations on what may be achieved by political means, but partly because man is an imperfect creature with a streak of evil as well as good in his inmost nature. By bitter experience Conservatives know that there are almost no limits to the misery of degradation to which bad governments may sink and depress their victims. But while others extol the virtues of the particular brand of Utopia they propose to create, the Conservative disbelieves them all, and, despite all temptations, offers in their place no Utopia at all but something quite modestly better than the present. He may, and should, have a programme. He certainly has . . . a policy. But of catchwords, slogans, visions, ideal states of society, classless societies, new orders, of all the tinsel and finery with which modern political charlatans charm their jewels from the modern political savage, the Conservative has nothing to offer. . . .

The aim of politics, as of all else, is the good life. But the good life is something which cannot be comprehended in some phrase or formula about any political or social order, and even if it could be so comprehended it could not be brought about, in the main, by political means. The Conservative contends that the most a politician can do is to ensure that some, and these by no means the most important, conditions in which the good life can exist are present, and, more important still, to prevent fools or knaves from setting up conditions which make an approach to the good life impossible except for solitaries or anchorites. A depressing creed? A negative creed? No! A Holy Gospel! All the great evils of our time have come from men who mocked and exploited human misery by pretending that good government, that is government according to their way of thinking, could offer Utopia.

(v) *The Wind of the Spirit*

The following passage is taken from an essay called "The Conservative attitude and Conservative social Policy" which Lord Eustace Percy contributed in 1935 to a volume under the title *Conservatism and the Future*.

Conservatism finds the motive force of human progress, not in the compulsory authority of the State, but in the individual's conscience and sense of duty. It is the individual human heart that is shaken by the wind of the Spirit. That wind can, no doubt, blow on governments, but only indirectly, and it can never blow through them. It blows through the " natural " society of the family, through the voluntary associations in which men band themselves together for mutual help and instruction, through organs of spiritual authority unarmed with any weapon of compulsion. Many of the greatest crimes and the greatest failures of history have been due to the attempt to realise the highest human ideals through political authority. . . .

This dualism, this belief in a *civitas dei* distinct from the political State, is the essential strength of Toryism, but it is also the reason why its political action seems often to be so unsatisfying. It will always remain true that the Tory will look outside politics for the fulfilment of many of his highest ideals.

(vi) *Laws reach but a very little way* . . .

Burke was the first Conservative thinker of any eminence to penetrate beneath the surface of laws and constitutions to the spirit of society and the personal qualities of individual men which give them their life and character. His criticism of the British Government's handling of the American Colonies was really a sustained plea for the spirit of the law against its letter. Similarly, in his attack on what he considered to be a corrupt Court-cabal which was degrading and confusing the government of his country in the early years of the reign of George III, he distrusted such remedies as constitutional reform or rearrangement and insisted that the true remedy lay in the employment of public men of character and integrity. The following statement of this view is taken from *Thoughts on the Causes of the Present Discontents* (1770).

Nations are not primarily ruled by laws . . . Nations are governed by the same methods, and on the same principles by which an individual without authority is often able to govern those who are his equals or his superiors; by a knowledge of their temper and by a judicious management of it. . . . The laws reach but a very little way. Constitute government how you please, infinitely the greater part of it must depend upon the exercise of the powers which are left at large to the prudence and uprightness of ministers of state. Even all the use and potency of the laws depend upon them. Without them, your commonwealth is no better than a scheme upon paper; not a living, active, effective constitution.

(vii) *The supposed "Talismanic" influence of Government*

By 1798, experience had taught Coleridge that " A Jacobin . . . is one who believes . . . that all or the greater part of the happiness or misery, virtue or vice, of mankind depends on forms of government . . ." and that this was a heresy unsupported by history and common sense. The following passage from a letter to his brother shows how, in the evolution of a Conservative outlook, he came to modify, even to reverse, this view. (*Letters of S. T. Coleridge*, ed. by E. H. Coleridge: April 1798).

One good consequence which I expect from revolution is that individuals will see the necessity of individual effort; that they will act as good Christians, rather than as citizens and electors; and so by degrees will purge off . . . the error of attributing to governments a talismanic influence over our virtues and our happiness, as if governments were not rather effects than causes. It is true that all effects react and become causes, and so it must be in some degree with governments; but there are other agents which act more powerfully because by a nigher and more continuous agency, and it remains true that governments are more the *effect than the cause of that which we are.*

(viii) *The Empire of Circumstance*

Burke's *Reflections on the Revolution in France* (1790) is the classic authority for the Aristotelian attitude to politics in modern times, and the following passages illustrate typically the attack upon "political arithmetic" which has become part of the Conservative tradition.

The world of contingency and political combination is much larger than we are apt to imagine. We can never say what may or may not happen, without a view to all the actual circumstances. Experience, upon other data than those, is of all things the most delusive. Prudence in new cases can do nothing on grounds of retrospect. A constant vigilance and attention to the train of things as they successively emerge, and to act on what they direct, are the only sure courses. . . .

I cannot . . . give praise or blame to anything which relates to human actions, and human concerns, on a simple view of the object as it stands stripped of every relation, in all the nakedness and solitude of metaphysical abstraction. Circumstances . . . give in reality to every political principle its distinguishing colour and discriminating effect. The circumstances are what render every civil and political scheme beneficial or noxious to mankind. . . .

I do not vilify theory and speculation—no, because that would be to vilify reason itself. . . . No, whenever I speak against theory, I mean always a weak, erroneous, fallacious, unfounded, or imperfect theory; and one of the ways of discovering that it is a false theory is by comparing it with practice. This is the true touchstone of all theories which regard man and the affairs of men—does it suit his nature in general—does it suit his nature as modified by his habits? . . .

Then what is the standard of expedience? Expedience is that which is good for the community, and good for every individual in it.

(ix) *Universal theories and National peculiarities*

Disraeli wrote his *Vindication of the English Constitution* in 1835, within a year of the triumph of Utilitarian principles in the Poor Law Amendment Act. In criticising the Utilitarians, Disraeli was carrying on the campaign, launched by Burke and supported by Coleridge, against the English exponents of Jacobinism, the latest school of ideologues to base their political and social teaching upon "abstract principles of theoretic science". Disraeli maintains that the only principles on which the government of a nation should be based are principles derived from a study of the nation's history: that is, on "certain principles of ancestral conduct" derived from historical observation of the national character in action.

The great object of our new school of statesmen ... is to form political institutions on abstract principles of theoretic science, instead of permitting them to spring from the course of events, and to be naturally created by the necessities of nations. It would appear that this scheme originated in the fallacy of supposing that theories produce circumstances, whereas the very converse of this proposition is correct and circumstances indeed produce theories. . . .

There are great crises in the fortunes of an ancient people which impel them to examine the nature of the institutions which have gradually sprung up amongst them. In this great national review, duly and wisely separating the essential character of their history from that which is purely adventitious, they discover certain principles of ancestral conduct which they acknowledge as the causes that these institutions have descended to them; and in their future career and all changes, reforms and alterations that they deem expedient, they resolve that these principles shall be their guide and their instructors. By these examinations they become deeply intimate with their national character; and on this increased knowledge, and on this alone, they hold it wise to act. This ... I hold to be the greatest amount of theory that ever enters into those political institutions which from their permanency are alone entitled to the consideration of a philosophical statesman: and this moderate, prudent, sagacious and eminently practical application of principles to conduct has ever been in the old time the illustrious characteristic of our English politicians.

(x) *The Child of Time*

Man is the child not only of circumstance but of time, and a certain attitude towards time, or towards the time-process which is change, is one of the distinguishing marks of Conservatism. The statesman ought always to be deeply aware that behind the circumstances or the situation in which he is called upon to act, or to refrain from acting, there lies the whole complex of human history, and more especially the peculiar history of his own country.

The present section puts together some of the best-known aphorisms of Burke on this subject.

A nation is not an idea only of local extent and individual momentary aggregation, but it is an idea of continuity which extends in time as well as in numbers and in space.

People will not look forwards to posterity, who never look backward to their ancestors.

By the unbridled facility of changing the state as often, and as much, and in as many ways, as their

floating fancies or fashions, the whole chain and continuity of the commonwealth would be broken. No
generation could link with the other. Men would
become little better than the flies of a summer.

We procure reverence to our civil institutions on the
principle upon which nature teaches us to revere
individual men; on account of their age, and on
account of those from whom they are descended.

By adhering in this manner and on those principles
to our forefathers, we are guided not by the superstitions
of antiquarians, but by the spirit of philosophical
analogy. . . .

(xi) *Disraeli sums up on " Time "*
The following passage from Disraeli's *Vindication of the
English Constitution* (1835) adds nothing to the tradition, but
it has significance as evidence of how the mind of the greatest
maker of the Conservative tradition in the nineteenth century
harked back to Burke.

This respect for precedent, this clinging to prescription, this reverence for antiquity, which are so often
ridiculed by conceited and superficial minds, and move
the special contempt of the gentlemen who admire
abstract principles, appear to me to have their origin
in a profound knowledge of human nature and in a
fine observation of public affairs, and satisfactorily
account for the permanent character of our liberties.
Those great men who have periodically risen to guide
the helm of our government in times of tumultuous
and stormy exigency, knew that a state is a complicated
creation of refined art, and they handled it with all
the delicacy the exquisite machinery requires. They

knew that if once they admitted the abstract rights of subjects, they must inevitably advance to the abstract rights of men, and then the very foundations of their civil polity would sink beneath them. . . . It is to this deference for what Lord Coke called reverend antiquity that I ascribe the duration of our commonwealth, and it is the spirit that has prevented even our revolutions from being destructive. . . .

I do not see, my Lord, that this reverence for antiquity has checked the progress of knowledge or stunted the growth of liberty in this island. We are universally held to be the freest people in Europe, and to have enjoyed our degree of freedom for a longer period than any existing state. . . . Assuredly this *summum bonum* is not to be found ensconced behind a revolutionary barricade, or floating in the bloody gutters of an incendiary metropolis. It cannot be scribbled down — this great invention — in a morning on the envelope of a letter by some charter-concocting monarch, or sketched with ludicrous facility in the conceited commonplace book of a Utilitarian sage. With us it has been the growth of ages, and brooding centuries have watched over and tended its perilous birth and feeble infancy.

CHAPTER 2

THE BODY POLITIC

To the Conservative, the state is not the product of artifice, convention, contract, conscious will and design; it is the product of nature and of time. Men do not elect to belong to it; they find themselves within it. It is natural because it answers to, and is the result of, man's terrestrial needs.

Because it is a growth of nature, it is organic and possesses a "character". Conservatism accepts the organic state as the political expression of the historic nation, and therefore accepts the concept of national character as a spirit of time and place.

The life of a society finds its primary and most ancient expression in the family, the church, and voluntary associations. The state is the ground-plan and the arbiter, not the origin or creator, of these.

Finally, Conservatism insists that the state is not a sacramental and compendious term for the whole range of social action, but is rather to be equated with "The Government"—which is a short-hand expression for those men who, for the time being and within limits, are entrusted by the community with the exercise of public force.

(i) *The State as Natural, not Artificial*

Burke must always be the primary Conservative authority on the state as a natural phenomenon, because in his *Reflections* he was concerned to assert just this natural and historical character of the state against a school of politicians who, he imagined, were engaged in the fruitless task of trying to create a state *de novo*. In his positive teaching he is, of course, generalising from the English state and the English Constitution.

Our constitution is a prescriptive constitution; it is a constitution whose sole authority is, that it has existed

time out of mind ... It is a better presumption even of
the *choice* of a nation, far better than any sudden and
temporary arrangement by actual election. Because a
nation is not only an idea of local extent and individual
momentary aggregation, but it is an idea of continuity
which extends in time as well as in numbers and space.
And this is a choice not of one day, or one set of people,
not a tumultuary and giddy choice; it is a deliberate
election of ages and of generations; it is a constitution
made by what is ten thousand times better than choice.
It is made by the peculiar circumstances, occasions,
tempers, dispositions, and moral, social and civil habi-
tudes of the people, which disclose themselves only in
a long space of time.

(ii) *A Historic Partnership*

Burke rejected the legalistic notion of the contractual origin
of state and government which had dominated the seventeenth
and eighteenth centuries, in favour of an idea of natural and
historic partnership in society. If we are to retain the idea of
contract at all, he would say, we must conceive of it, in the case
of any particular state, as a symbol of the inviolable compact
which holds all moral and physical natures together in the grand
design of the universe. When he had carried the conception on
to this plane, he had shorn it of all legalistic meaning: turned
it, in fact, from an instrument of revolutionary change into a
quasi-divine sanction of the existing order of things.

The passage given below is from the *Reflections*.

Society is indeed a contract. Subordinate contracts
for objects of mere occasional interest may be dissolved
at pleasure—but the state ought not to be considered
nothing better than a partnership agreement in a trade
of pepper and coffee, calico or tobacco, or some other
such low concern, to be taken up for a little temporary
interest, and to be dissolved by the fancy of the parties.

It is to be looked on with other reverence; because it is not a partnership in things subservient only to the gross animal existence of a temporary and perishable nature. It is a partnership in all science; a partnership in all art; a partnership in every virtue, and in all perfection. As the ends of such a partnership cannot be obtained in many generations, it becomes a partnership not only between those who are living, but between those who are living, those who are dead, and those who are to be born.

Each contract of each particular state is but a clause in the great primeval contract of eternal society, linking the lower with the higher natures, connecting the visible and invisible world, according to a fixed compact sanctioned by the inviolable oath which holds all physical and all moral natures, each in their appointed place. This law is not subject to the will of those who, by an obligation above them, and infinitely superior, are bound to submit their will to that law. The municipal corporations of that universal kingdom are not morally at liberty at their pleasure, and on their speculations of a contingent improvement, wholly to separate and tear asunder the bands of their subordinate community, and to dissolve it into an unsocial, uncivil, unconnected chaos of elementary principles. It is the first and supreme necessity only, a necessity that is not chosen but chooses, a necessity paramount to deliberation, that admits no discussion and demands no evidence, which alone can justify a resort to anarchy. This necessity is no exception to the rule; because this necessity is a part too of that moral and physical disposition of things, to which man must be obedient by consent or force; but if that which is only submission to necessity should be made the object of choice, the

law is broken, nature is disobeyed, and the rebellious
are outlawed, cast forth, and exiled, from this world
of reason and order, and peace, and virtue, and fruitful penitence, into the antagonist world of madness,
discord, vice, confusion, and unavailing sorrow.

(iii) *Contract redeemed as an " Idea "*

In the splendid passage just quoted, Burke raised the notion
of contract to a philosophical plane, no doubt with the intention
to render it harmless. He had made it into a symbol of the
divinely appointed order of things, or of a law of cohesion in the
nature of things which even God Himself observes. Coleridge,
while likewise rejecting it as a historical reality and exposing the
moral fallacy involved in it, yet was prepared to accept it as the
symbol of an " Idea ". His elucidation of the philosophic " Idea "
of the Social Contract led him to set forth what is, perhaps, the
leading principle of the Conservative tradition of political obligation: the principle that " a *person* can never, but by his own
fault, become a *thing*, or, without grievous wrong be treated as
such ".

The text is from the first chapter of *The Constitution of the
Church and State according to the Idea of Each* (1830).

Every reader of Rousseau, or of Hume's Essays, will
understand me when I refer to the Original Social
Contract, assumed by Rousseau, and by other and
wiser men before him, as the basis of all legitimate
government. Now, if this be taken as the assertion of
an historical fact, or as the application of a conception
generalised from ordinary compacts between man and
man, or nation and nation, to an actual occurrence in
the first ages of the world; namely, the formation of
the first contract in which men covenanted with each
other to associate, or in which a multitude entered into
a compact with a few, the one to be governed, the other
to govern, under certain declared conditions: I shall run
little hazard at this time of day in declaring the

pretended fact a pure fiction, and the conception of such a fact an idle fancy. It is at once false and foolish. For what if an original contract had actually been entered into and formally recorded? Still I cannot see what addition of moral force would be gained by the fact. The same sense of moral obligation which binds us to keep it must have pre-existed in the same force and in relation to the same duties, impelling our ancestors to make it. For what could it do more than bind the contracting parties to act for the general good, according to their best lights and opportunities? It is evident that no specific scheme or constitution can derive any other claim to our reverence than that which the presumption of its fitness for the general good shall give it; and which claim of course ceases, or rather is reversed, as soon as this presumption of its utility has given place to as general a conviction to the contrary. It is true, indeed, that from duties anterior to the formation of the contract, because they arise out of the very constitution of our humanity, which supposes the social state—it is true, that in order to a rightful removal of the institution or law thus agreed on, it is required that the conviction of its expediency shall be as general as the presumption of its fitness was at the time of its establishment. This, the first of the two great paramount interests of the social state demands, namely that of permanence; but to attribute more than this to any fundamental articles passed into law by an assembly of individuals, is an injustice to their successors and a high offence against the other great interest of the social state—namely, its progressive improvement. The conception, therefore, of an original contract, is, we repeat, incapable of historic proof as a fact, and it is senseless as a theory.

But if instead of a *conception* or *theory* of an original social contract, you say the *idea* of an ever-originating social contract, this is so certain and so indispensable that it constitutes the whole ground of the difference between subject and serf, between a commonwealth and a slave-plantation. . .

And this again is evolved out of the yet higher idea of *person*, in contra-distinction from *thing*,—all social law and justice being grounded on the principle that a person can never, but by his own fault, become a *thing*, or, without grievous wrong, be treated as such: and the distinction consisting in this, that a thing may be used altogether and merely as a *means* to an end; but the person must always be included in the *end*: his interest must form a part of the *object*, a means to which he, by consent, i.e. by his own act, makes himself.

(iv) *The State as an Organism*

Conservatives accept the analogy between the Body Politic and the Body Natural as imperfect but illuminating. The analogy must be used with caution, and simply as a means of illustrating the interdependence of the members of a political society.

The first paragraph below is taken from Coleridge's " Table Talk ", December 18, 1831. The second is from *Notes* (Omniana). The third is from *The Friend* (Section I, Political Knowledge, Essay 14).

The difference between an inorganic and an organic body lies in this: in the first—a sheaf of corn—the whole is nothing more than a collection of the individual parts or phenomena. In the second—a man—the whole is everything and the parts are nothing. A State is an idea intermediate between the two, the whole being a result from, and not a mere total of, the parts,

—and yet not so merging the constituent parts in the result, but that the individual exists integrally within it.

Unlike a million of tigers, a million of men is very different from one man. Each man in a numerous society is not only co-existent with, but virtually organised into, the multitude of which he is an integral part. His *idem* is modified by the *alter*. And there arise impulses and objects from this *synthesis* of the *alter et idem*, myself and my neighbour. This again is strictly analogous to what takes place in the vital organisation of the individual man.

The true patriot will reverence not only whatever tends to make the component individuals more happy, and more worthy of happiness; but likewise whatever tends to bind them together more closely as a people: that as a multitude of parts and functions make up one human body, so the whole multitude of his countrymen may, by the visible and invisible influences of religion, language, laws, customs, and the reciprocal dependence and reaction of trade and agriculture, be organised into one body politic. But much as he desires to see *all* become a whole, he places limits even to this wish, and abhors that system of policy which would blend men into a state by the dissolution of all those virtues which make them happy and estimable as individuals.

(v) *National Personality*

The transition from the organic view of the state to a theory of national personality, or character, may be illustrated by the following excerpt from Gladstone's *The State in its Relations with the Church*, which was published in 1838, when its author was " the hope of those stern unbending Tories ".

The plainest exposition of national personality is this—that a nation fulfils the great condition of a person: namely, that it has unity of acting, and unity of suffering; with the difference that what is physically single in the one, is joint, or morally single, in the other. . . . There are qualities in a combination which arise not out of the union of its parts, and are not to be found in the parts taken singly when resolved into their separate state. Such a combination we find in the government and laws of a country: not a mere aggregation of individual acts, but a composite agency of many, each of whose separate efforts in part modifies, in part is blended with, the rest, and issues in a result which is the act of the nation in its collective personality. It is this composite agency which . . . has a being. . . .

(vi) *The Soul of a Nation*

The theory of national character, although it was already evolving in the eighteenth century at the hands of students of philology and folk-lore like Herder, was a characteristic element in the English romantic Movement. Burke had upheld nationality in America, Ireland and Poland, but it was the Lake Poets—inspired immediately by the national uprising of the Spaniards against Napoleon—who really voiced the doctrine in the spiritual form familiar to the nineteenth century. Obviously it is no monopoly of Conservative thinkers, but it was by Conservatives like Wordsworth and Coleridge that it found its noblest and most natural expression.

The following is a passage from Coleridge's *Letters on the Spaniards*, which appeared in *The Courier* in 1810, and are reprinted in his *Essays on His Own Times*, edited by Sara Coleridge (1850).

That there is an individual spirit that breathes through a whole people, is participated in by all, though not by all alike; a spirit which gives a colour and character to their virtues and vices, so that the same actions . . . are yet not the same in a Spaniard as they would be in a Frenchman, I hold for an undeniable truth, without the admission of which all history would be riddle. I hold likewise that the difference of nations, their relative grandeur and meanness, all, in short, which they are or do . . . all in which they persevere as a nation, through successive generations of changing individuals, are the result of this spirit.

(vii) *The Solemn Fraternity of a Great Nation*

After the defeat of Marshal Junot by Sir Arthur Wellesley at Vimeiro in 1808, the British Government signed the Convention of Cintra, by which the French received very lenient terms on their withdrawal from Portugal. Many English patriots held that we had betrayed the insurgent peoples of the Peninsula, and Wordsworth wrote his famous tract, *On the Convention of Cintra*, in 1809, one of the cardinal documents in the evolution of the theory of nationality and national self-determination. In the following passage he is deploring the ignorance of routine statesmen on the depth and power of national feeling.

The instincts of natural and social man; the deeper emotions; the simpler feelings; the spacious range of the disinterested imagination; the pride in country for country's sake, when to serve has not been a formal profession—and the mind is therefore left in a state of dignity only to be surpassed by having served nobly and generously; the instantaneous accomplishment in which they start up who, upon a searching call, stir for the land which they love—not from personal motives, but for a reward which is undefined and cannot be missed: the solemn fraternity which a great nation composes—gathered together, in a stormy season, under the shade of ancestral feeling; the delicacy of moral honour which pervades the minds of a people when despair has been suddenly thrown off and expectations are lofty; . . . these arrangements and resources of nature, these ways and means of society, have so little connection with those others upon which a ruling minister of a long established government is accustomed to depend; these—elements as it were of a universe, functions of a living body,—are so opposite in their mode of action to the formal machine which it has been his pride to manage;—that he has but a faint perception of their immediate efficacy; knows not the facility· with which they assimilate with other powers; nor the property by which such of them as, from the necessity of nature, must change or pass away, will, under wise and fearless management, surely generate lawful successors to fill their place when their appropriate work is performed.

(viii) *What makes a Nation*

We have already seen something of Disraeli's thought on nationality in Chapter I, section xi. He equated national character with those " principles of ancestral conduct " which are revealed in a people's history. The theme is developed in the passages given below. The first paragraph is taken from *The Vindication of the English Constitution* (1835); the second and fourth from *The Spirit of Whiggism* (1834); the third from *The Runnymede Letters* (1836).

If we survey the career of an individual, we shall on the whole observe a remarkable consistency in his conduct; yet it is more than possible that this individual has never acted from that organised philosophy which we style system. What then has produced this consistency? His individual character. Nations have characters as well as individuals. . . . The ruling passion which is the result of organisation regulates the career of an individual subject to those superior accidents of fortune whose secondary influence is scarcely inferior to the impulse of his nature. The blended influences of nature and fortune form his character; 'tis the same with nations.

A nation is a work of art and a work of time. A nation is gradually created by a variety of influences—the influence of original organisation, of climate, soil, religion, customs, manners, extraordinary accidents and incidents in their history, and the individual character of their illustrious citizens. These influences create the nation—these form the national mind. . . .

A nation is not a mere mass of bipeds with no strength but their animal vigour, and no collective grandeur but that of their numbers. There is required to constitute that great creation, a people, some higher endowments and some rarer—honour and faith and justice; a national spirit fostered by national exploits; a solemn creed expounded by a pure and learned priesthood; a jurisprudence which is the aggregate wisdom of ages; the spirit of chivalry, the inspiration of religion, the supremacy of law; that free order and that natural gradation of ranks which are but a type and image of the economy of the universe; a love of home and country, fostered by traditionary manners and consecrated by customs that embalm ancestral deeds; learned establishments, the institutions of charity; a skill in refined and useful arts; the discipline of fleets and armies; and above all, a national character, serious and yet free: a character neither selfish nor conceited, but which is conscious that as it owes much to its ancestors, so also it will not stand acquitted if it neglect its posterity—these are some of the incidents and qualifications of a great nation like the people of England.

That great body corporate, styled a nation,—a vast assemblage of human beings knit together by laws and arts and customs, by the necessities of the present and the memory of the past. . . .

(ix) *Man v. the State: an unreal antithesis*

The following passage from Kenneth Pickthorn's essay, *Principles and Prejudices* (Signpost Books, 1943), speaks for itself. It is a fine example of the essentially concrete treatment of a problem that is generally wrongly stated because it is stated in terms of antithesis: a representative Conservative treatment.

Whether a man was made for the State, or the State for man, is not the most urgent of questions because it it not perfectly certain that it means anything. Man, in any sense which matters to this discussion, means an animal, part of whose essence is society; and, even more clearly, there can be no human society that does not consist of men and exist for them. Socialism and Individualism, like every other heresy, err by over-insistence upon something that is true. Between two truths, either of which swallowed whole is a lie, the Conservative will not choose; he will reject neither, and will not bolt either whole; but with the help of certain habits of mind he may hope to get some nourishment from both, without poison from either.

When he thinks of himself as a private individual, he will require no unusual degree of unselfish virtue, but only a slightly heightened self-consciousness, to think of himself, not as a complete unit which can be isolated, but as a member of this family and of that trade union, a shareholder perhaps in one company and a subscriber to a benefit society, a trustee here and a beneficiary there. He has a multiplicity of personages, and the whole of him goes into no one of them more than momentarily. If there is one He which includes and transcends all the parts he plays, that is a He which escapes all material constraint and baffles all human calculation, a religious and not a political entity.

When he thinks of himself as a subject, one who pays taxes and obeys laws, he will require no more than ordinary devotion to the largest of the groups to which he belongs, his country with its constituted government, in order to persuade himself that he ought to give the benefit of every doubt to the State, to what gives organised and traditional direction to all his kin and friends and partners: in this sense, and to this extent, he will subordinate the individual to the State.

It is when he thinks of himself as a ruler, a sharer in government, that he needs most virtue if he is to keep individual and collectivity, State and subject, country and person, from antagonism, and even from competitiveness or contrast, in his mind. . . . It is much more difficult to remember every time you vote as a member of Parliament or a county councillor or an ordinary elector, or every time you speak or act in a way likely to influence those personages or similar personages; it is much more difficult to remember that on each of these occasions *you* are the State, or an active organ of it, that you ought therefore to have uppermost in your mind the paramount value of individuals, and ought to be sure that your speaking and acting are not directed to the interest of the one individual that is yourself, to the harnessing of society's horse, foot and guns to your plough, or worse still, to your own hobby, worst of all to your pet recipe for improving other people.

(x) *The Rights of Man*

When Conservatives speak of " Rights " they mean, or should mean, those rights which accrue to men from their membership of society; and those rights are the counterpart of duties. As Burke put it, rather more than a century and a half ago: " Men cannot enjoy the rights of an uncivil and of a civil state together."

This was expressed in classic form by Burke and Coleridge in the age of the French Revolution, when "natural rights " were the latest fashion.

The following passages are taken from the *locus classicus* for this question: Burke's *Reflections on the Revolution in France.*

Government is not made in virtue of natural rights, which may and do exist in total independence of it; and exist in much greater clearness, and in a much greater degree of abstract perfection; but their abstract perfection is their practical defect. By having a right to everything, they want everything. Government is a contrivance of human wisdom to provide for human *wants.* Men have a right that these wants should be provided for by this wisdom. Among these wants is to be reckoned the want, out of civil society, of a sufficient restraint upon their passions. Society requires not only that the passions of individuals should be subjected, but that even in the mass and body, as well as in the individuals, the inclinations of men should frequently be thwarted, their will controlled, and their passions brought into subjection. This can only be done *by a power out of themselves*; and not, in the exercise of its function, subject to that will and to those passions which it is its office to bridle and subdue. In this sense the restraints on men, as well as their liberties, are to be reckoned among their rights. But as the liberties and the restrictions vary with times and circumstances, and admit of infinite modifications, they cannot be settled upon any abstract rule; and nothing is so foolish as to discuss them upon that principle.

How can any man claim, under the conventions of civil society, rights which do not so much as suppose its existence?—rights which are absolutely repugnant to it? One of the first motives to civil society, and which becomes one of its fundamental rules, is, *that no man should be judge in his own cause*. By this each person has at once divested himself of the first fundamental right of uncovenanted man, that is, to judge for himself and to assert his own cause. He abdicates all right to be his own governor. He inclusively, in a great measure abandons the right of self-defence, the first law of nature. Men cannot enjoy the rights of an uncivil and of a civil state together. That he may obtain justice, he gives up his right of determining what it is in points the most essential to him. That he may secure some liberty, he makes a surrender in trust of the whole of it.

Far am I from denying in theory, full as far in my heart from withholding in practice (if I were of power to give or withhold) the *real* rights of men. In denying their false claims of right, I do not mean to injure those which are real, and are such as their pretended rights would totally destroy. If civil society be made for the advantage of man, all the advantages for which it is made become his right. It is an institution of beneficence; and law itself is only beneficence acting by a rule. Men have a right to live by that rule; they have a right to do justice, as between their fellows, whether their fellows are in politic function or in ordinary occupation. They have a right to the fruits of their industry; and to the means of making their industry fruitful. They have a right to the acquisitions of their parents; to the nourishment and improvement of their offspring; to instruction in life and consolation in death. Whatever each man can separately do, without trespassing upon others, he has a right to do for himself; and he has a right to a fair portion of all which society, with all its combinations of skill and force, can do in his favour. In this partnership all men have equal rights; but not to equal things. He that has but five shillings in the partnership, has as good a right to it as he that has five hundred pounds has to his larger proportion. But he has not a right to an equal dividend in the product of the joint stock; and as to the share of power, authority and direction which each individual ought to have in the management of the state, that I must deny to be amongst the direct original rights of man in civil society; for I have in my contemplation the civil social man, and no other. It is a thing to be settled by convention.

The pretended rights of these theorists are all extremes; and in proportion as they are metaphysically true, they are morally and politically false. The rights of men are in a sort of *middle*, incapable of definition, but not impossible to be discerned. The rights of men in governments are their advantages; and these are often in balances between differences of good; in compromises between good and evil, and sometimes between evil and evil. Political reasoning is a computing principle; adding, subtracting, multiplying, and dividing, morally, and not metaphysically or mathematically, true moral denominations.

(xi) *Rights and Duties*

Coleridge's numerous statements on the interdependence of rights and duties afford as useful a statement of the traditional

Conservative position as could be found anywhere. Unfortunately, these statements are ·scattered in widely separated parts of his works, and the following section represents an attempt to construct a patchwork.

The component parts are taken from " Table Talk ", November 20, 1831; *The Statesman's Manual* (1816); *Essays on His Own Times*, ed. by Sara   Coleridge (1850), Vol. II, pp. 542–562; and *Two Addresses on Sir Robert Peel's Bill* (1818), ed. by Edmund Gosse (1913).

Rights! There are no rights whatever without corresponding duties. . . . When the government and the aristocracy of this country had subordinated *persons* to *things*, and treated the one like the other, the poor, with some reason, learned to set up *rights* above duties. Look at the history of the growth of our Constitution, and you will see that our ancestors never upon any occasion stated, as a ground for claiming any of their privileges, an abstract right inherent in themselves; you will nowhere in our parliamentary records find the miserable sophism of the Rights of Man. No! They were too wise for that. They took good care to refer their claims to custom and prescription, and boldly—sometimes very impudently—asserted them upon traditionary and constitutional grounds. . . .

English subjects . . . pretend to no *rights* that do not refer to some *duty* as their origin and true foundation. . . . Right, in its most proper sense, is the creature of law and statute, and only in the technical language of the courts has it any substantial and independent sense. In morals, right is a word without meaning except as the co-relative of duty. . . . Whoever builds a government on personal and natural rights is so far a Jacobin. Whoever builds on social rights, that is, hereditary rank, property, and long prescription, is an anti-Jacobin, even though he should nevertheless be a republican or even a democrat. . . . Between the acknowledged truth that in all countries both governments and subjects have duties—duties both to themselves and to each other . . . between this truism and the Jacobinical doctrine of the universal inalienable right of all the inhabitants of every country to the exercise of their inherent sovereignty, there is no middle step, no middle meaning.

(xii) *Liberty and Law*

Conservatism rejects Liberty as an absolute, or the anarchic moral autonomy involved in "doing as one likes". Conservatism begins with Burke's aphorism: Liberty must be limited in order to be enjoyed. The first limitation on Liberty is a law in the mind: a law that tells us we have a *right* to do what we *ought* to do. Burke takes up the subject at the second stage: the limitation of liberty by municipal, or constitutional, law, although he does, as a Christian philosopher, insist that men's passions forge their fetters.

The following section is made up of three passages from Burke's speeches and writings. The first paragraph is from " A Letter from Mr. Burke to a Member of the French National Assembly " (1791); the second from his " Speech on Conciliation with America " (1775); the third from *Reflections on the Revolution in France* (1790).

Men are qualified for civil liberty in exact proportion to their disposition to put moral chains upon their own appetites; in proportion as their love to justice is above their rapacity; in proportion as their soundness and sobriety of understanding is above their vanity and presumption; in proportion as they are more disposed to listen to the counsels of the wise and good in preference to the flattery of knaves. Society cannot exist unless a controlling power upon will and appetite be placed somewhere, and the less of it there is within, the more of it there must be without. It is ordained in the eternal constitution of things that men of intemperate minds cannot be free. Their passions forge their fetters.

Abstract liberty, like other mere abstractions, is not to be found. Liberty inheres in some sensible object. . . .

I flatter myself that I love a manly, moral, regulated liberty. . . . But I cannot stand forward and give praise or blame to anything which relates to human actions and human concerns, on a simple view of the object. . . . Abstractedly speaking, government, as well as liberty, is good. . . . When I see the spirit of liberty in action, I see a strong principle at work; and this, for a while, is all I can possibly know of it. . . . I should therefore suspend my congratulations [until I can see how this liberty has] been combined with government; with public force; with the discipline and obedience of armies; with the collection of an effective and well-distributed revenue; with morality and religion; with solidity and property; with peace and order; with civil and social manners. All these (in their way) are good things, too; and without them liberty is not a benefit while it lasts, and is not likely to continue long. The effect of liberty to individuals is, that they may do what they please: we ought to see what it will please them to do before we risk congratulations, which may be soon turned into complaints. Prudence would dictate this in the case of separate, insulated, private men; but liberty, when men act in bodies, is *power*. Considerate people, before they declare themselves, will observe the use which is made of *power*; and particularly of so trying a thing as *new* power in *new* persons. . . .

(xiii) *A Contemporary Statement*

Almost any modern Conservative publicist might be quoted for the enunciation of the traditional principle that law and liberty are not enemies but reciprocal forces in a politically organised society. The following passage is taken from Mr. Quintin Hogg's *The Case for Conservatism* (1947).

Conservatives believe in variety and liberty of development under the rule of law. Law they regard as something neither the enemy of liberty nor of authority, but reconciling both. Law is the means of robbing liberty of its anarchic tendencies, and removing from authority the elements of caprice. Law must be public, law must be of general application, law must be reasonable, law must be constitutionally enacted after open discussion, impartially administered, uncorruptly enforced. Given these characteristics there is no conflict between liberty and authority. Authority is simply the name we give to the organs of government entrusted with the duty of protecting the rights and liberties of all, accorded by law, from the caprices or whims of each, and liberty the rights and powers that each expects will be respected and accorded by all in return for a similar forbearance from himself. Law is the name we give to the liberties of others which we must respect if we expect to receive the like ourselves.

CHAPTER 3

POWER AND RESPONSIBILITY

Where does political authority come from, and to whom, or to what, is it responsible?

Conservatism has never accepted the notion that political authority is derived from, or responsible to, some determinate political entity with a " Will "—such as " the greatest number ", or " the People ". Government, to the Conservative, is not based on Will but on Reason. " If government were a matter of will upon any side," Burke told the electors of Bristol, " without question yours ought to be superior. But government and legislation are matters of reason and judgment, and not of inclination. . . ." This is fully illustrated in the first chapter of Part II of this book.

To the Conservative, the authority of law depends upon its consonance with reason. The statesman is obliged (quoting Burke again) to subject " occasional will to permanent reason . . . to the steady maxims of faith, justice, and fixed fundamental policy ".

Conservatism finds the pledges of responsibility on the part of men entrusted with authority, in the personal character and public repute of the individual politician. It persists in the old-fashioned notion that the possession of a certain amount of property is some guarantee, though not the only one, that a man is prudent, practical and reasonably far-sighted. To the Conservative, this is a more tangible, if less emotionally satisfying, theory of responsibility than the Radical theory of the General Will or the Socialist theory of the Mandate.

(i) *All Power is a Trust*

In his *Reflections on the Revolution in France*, Burke insisted that the people might be just as wrong as Kings and Aristocrats. The value of his teaching, stripped of its panic and prejudice,

for Conservatism, lies in his clear insistence upon two things:
(1) that the power of the people is no less a trust than the power
of princes; and (2) that numbers do not necessarily make for
right, and even less for righteousness.

The first three paragraphs below are from the *Reflections*, and
the fourth is from a speech to his Bristol constituents before the
election of 1780.

All persons possessing any portion of power ought to
be strongly and most awfully impressed with the idea
that they act in trust; and that they are to account for
their conduct in that trust to the one great Master,
Author and Founder of Society.

This principle ought to be even more strongly impressed upon the minds of those who compose the
collective sovereignty than upon those of single
princes. . . . Where popular authority is absolute and
unrestrained, the people have an infinitely greater,
because a far better founded, confidence in their own
power. They are themselves, in a great measure, their
own instruments. They are nearer to their objects.
Besides, they are less under responsibility to one of
the greatest controlling powers on earth, the sense of
fame and estimation. The share of infamy that is likely
to fall to the lot of each individual in public acts is
small indeed; the operation of opinion being in the
inverse ratio to the number of those who abuse power.
Their own approbation of their own acts has to them
the appearance of a public judgment in their favour.
A perfect democracy is, therefore, the most shameless
thing in the world. As it is the most shameless, it is
also the most fearless. No man apprehends in his person
that he can be made subject to punishment. Certainly
the people at large never ought: for as all punishments
are for an example towards the conservation of the
people at large, the people at large can never become

the subject of punishments by any human hand. It is therefore of infinite importance that they should not be suffered to imagine that their will, any more than that of kings, is the standard of right and wrong. They ought to be persuaded that they are full as little entitled, and far less qualified, to use any arbitrary power whatever.

It is said that twenty-four millions ought to prevail over two hundred thousand. True; if the constitution of a kingdom be a problem in arithmetic. This sort of discourse does well enough with the lamp-post for its second: to men who *may* reason calmly, it is ridiculous. The will of the many, and their interest, must very often differ; and great will be the difference when they make an evil choice. . . .

As to the opinion of the people, which some think . . . is to be implicitly obeyed. . . . When we know that the opinions of even the greatest multitudes are the standard of rectitude, I shall think myself obliged to make those opinions the masters of my conscience. But if it may be doubted whether Omnipotence itself is competent to alter the essential constitution of right and wrong, sure I am, that such *things* as they and I, are possessed of no such power. No man carries further than I do the policy of making government pleasing to the people. But the widest range of this politic complaisance is confined within the limits of justice.

(ii) *Vox Populi, vox Dei?*

Coleridge puts the answer to this question succinctly in two passages of his " Table Talk " (April 29, 1832, and November 20, 1831) which might stand as a summary of the Conservative view.

I never said that the *vox populi* was, of course, the *vox dei*. It may be; but it may be, with equal probability, *a priori, vox diaboli.* That the voice of ten millions of men calling for the same thing is a spirit, I believe; but whether that be a spirit of Heaven or Hell, I can only know by trying the thing called for by the prescript of reason and God's will. . . . I believe that the feeling of the multitude will, in most cases, be in favour of something good; but this it is which I perceive, that they are always under the domination of some one feeling or view; whereas truth, and above all, practical wisdom, must be the result of a wide comprehension of the more and the less, the balance and the counter-balance.

(iii) *The Credentials of the Legislator:* (1) *Character*
Conservative thinkers, perhaps because they have been bred in a country with a great aristocratic tradition, where character has always been preferred to intellect (although intellect has not been despised), have always laid great emphasis on the element of personality in politics. They have tended to argue that the best safeguard for the responsible use of power is the upright character of public men. From Burke's *Reflections on the Revolution in France:*

Men are in public life as in private, some good, some bad. . . . No name, no power, no function, no artificial institution whatsoever, can make the men of whom any system of authority is composed, any other than God, and nature, and education, and their habits of life have made them. Capacities beyond these the people have not to give. Virtue and wisdom may be the objects of their choice; but their choice confers neither the one nor the other on those upon whom they confer their ordaining hands.

Every good political institution must have a preventive operation as well as a remedial. It ought to have a natural tendency to exclude bad men from government. . . . Before men are put forward into the great trusts of the state, they ought by their conduct to have obtained such a degree of estimation in their country as may be some sort of pledge and security to the public that they will not abuse those trusts. It is no mean security for a proper use of power, that a man has shown by the general tenour of his actions that the affection, the good opinion, the confidence of his fellow-citizens have been among the principal objects of his life. . . .

It is therefore our business carefully to cultivate our minds, to rear to the most perfect vigour and maturity every sort of generous and honest feeling that belongs to our nature. To bring the dispositions that are lovely in private life into the service and conduct of the commonwealth; so to be patriots, as not to forget we are gentlemen. . . . Public life is a situation of power and energy; he trespasses against his duty who sleeps upon his watch, as well as he that goes over to the enemy.

There is no qualification for government but virtue and wisdom, actual or presumptive. Wherever they are actually found, they have, in whatever state, condition, profession or trade, the passport of heaven to human place and honour. . . . Nothing is a due and adequate representation of a state that does not represent its ability as well as its property. . . . Woe to the country which would madly and impiously reject the service of the talents and virtues, civil, military, or religious, that are given to grace and to serve it; and would condemn to obscurity everything formed to diffuse lustre and glory around a state. Woe to that country, too, that passing to the opposite extreme, considers a low education, a mean contracted view of things, a sordid mercenary occupation, as a preferable title to command. Everything ought to be open; but not indifferently to every man. No rotation; no appointment by lot; no mode of election operating in a spirit of sortition or rotation can be generally good in a government conversant in extensive objects. . . . I do not hesitate to say that the road to eminence and power, from obscure condition, ought not to be made too easy, nor a thing too much of course. If rare merit be the rarest of all rare things, it ought to pass through some sort of probation. The temple of honour ought to be seated on an eminence. If it be opened through virtue, let it·be remembered too that virtue is never tried but by some difficulty and some struggle.

(iv) *The Credentials of the Legislator:* (2) *Talent*
    not enough

Coleridge believed that there are two qualifications necessary for political eminence: an habitual interest in the great problems of philosophy, and the possession of some share in " the collective and registerable property " of the commonwealth. The only safeguard against the tyranny of planners, managers, and technocrats was, he held, to insist that talent be qualified in prudence and moderation by the possession of property. Conservatism endorses his criticism here, even if it questions the sufficiency of his solution.

The first paragraph below is taken from *The Statesman's Manual* (1816); the remainder, with the exception of the telling sentence about planners, which comes from the same source, and the passage allying modern philosophy with despotism, which comes from *Essays on his Own Time*, Vol. II, pp. 652–656, is taken from *The Church and State*, Chapter X.

The first man on whom the light of an idea dawned did in that same moment receive the spirit and credentials of a law-giver; and as long as man shall exist, so long will the possession of that antecedent knowledge . . . which exists only in the power of an idea, be the one lawful qualification of all dominion in the world of the senses.

Need I add the inherent unfitness, as well as the direful consequences, of making virtue . . . depend on talent—a gift so unequally dispensed by nature, the degree in which it is given being indeed different in every person, and the development and cultivation of which are affected by all the inequalities of fortune? This is one proof . . . among many, that there is a natural affinity between despotism and modern philosophy, notwithstanding the proud pretensions of the latter as the emancipator of the human race. . . . The *aristocracy* of talent is, therefore, no unmeaning phrase in itself, execrable as was its purport in the minds of its first framers: it exists . . . wherever the understanding, or calculating faculty, which is properly the executive branch of self-government, has usurped that supreme legislative power which belongs *jure divino* to our *moral* being. [Its consequence is] the general conceit that states and governments ought to be constructed as machines . . . the consequent multitude of plans and constitutions, of planners and constitution-makers, and the remorseless arrogance with which the authors and proselytes of every new proposal [are] ready to realise it, be the cost what it might in the established rights, or even the lives of men.

If superior talents, and the mere possession of knowledges such as can be learnt at Mechanics' Institutions, were regularly accompanied with a will in harmony with the reason, and a consequent subordination of the appetites and passions to the ultimate ends of our being; if intellectual gifts and attainments were infallible signs of wisdom and goodness in the same proportion, and the knowing, clever and *talented* (vile word!) were always *rational*; if the mere facts of science conferred or superseded the soft'ning humanising influences of the moral world . . . then, indeed, political power might not unwisely be conferred as the honorarium or privilege of having passed through all the forms of a National School, without the security of political ties, without those fastening and radical fibres of a collective and registerable property by which the citizen inheres in and belongs to the Commonwealth. . . . But as the contrary of all these suppositions may be more safely assumed, the practical conclusion will be . . . that the gifts of the understanding . . . should be allowed fair play in the acquiring of that proprietorship to which a certain portion of political power belongs as its proper function. For in this way there is at least a strong probability that intellectual power will be armed with political power only where it has previously been combined with and guarded by the moral qualities of prudence, industry and self-control.

(v) *The disease of excessive organisation*

When Conservatives protest against the tendency towards an excessive organisation of the life of the community, which seems to be a feature of Collectivist policy in all ages, they are not merely grumbling about "controls" of "officialdom", or pleading for "private enterprise" or *"laissez-faire"*. They are warning against the hardening of the arteries of the Body Politic which Coleridge diagnosed as a typical disease of democracies. An instinctive Tory like Cobbett could deplore the never ending recurrence to Acts of Parliament as early as 1803–5 (*Progress of a Ploughboy*, p. 105): "something must be left," he thought, "and something ought to be left, to the sense and reason and morality and religion of the people." An intellectual Tory like Coleridge, however, expressed the same thought in pathological terms in Chapters X and XI of his *Church and State* (1830), from which source the following passage is taken.

The first condition . . . required to a sound constitution of the Body Politic is a due proportion of the free and permeative life and energy of the Nation to the organised powers brought within containing channels. . . . What the exact proportion, however, of the two kinds of force should be it is impossible to predetermine. But the existence of a disproportion is sure to be detected sooner or later by the effects. Thus, the ancient Greek democracies, the hot-beds of Art, Science, Genius and Civilisation, fell into dissolution from the excess of the former, the permeative power deranging the functions, and by explosions shattering the organic structures they should have enlivened. On the contrary, the Republic of Venice fell by the contrary extremes. All political power was confined to the determinate vessels, and these, becoming more and more rigid, even to an ossification of the arteries, the State, in which the people were nothing, lost all power of resistance *ad extra.* . . . Extremes meet—an adage of inexhaustible exemplification. A democratic Republic and an Absolute Monarchy agree in this: that in both, the Nation or People delegates its whole power. Nothing is left obscure, nothing suffered to remain in the Idea, unevolved and only acknowledged as an existing, yet interminable Right. A Constitution such states can scarcely be said to possess. The whole Will of the Body Politic is in act at every moment.

(vi) *The Diffusion of Power:* (1) *Burke*

The distinctively Conservative contribution to the solution of the problem of combining power with responsibility is to be found in the principle of the diffusion of power. Tory philosophy evolved within a society where power was shared and diffused: English society in the eighteenth and early nineteenth centuries. It carries over the political philosophy of that older society into an age which has seen the conditions that bred it gradually undermined and dissolved in the centralised, bureaucratic "Great State".

Burke, in his *Reflections on the Revolution in France* (1790), analysed the constitutional structure imposed on France by the "political geometers" of the National Assembly, a structure which flattened out all the ancient irregularities of classes, corporations, estates, *parlements,* which had for so long stood in the way of an efficient despotism. He predicted that the result would be to put France at the mercy of the first military adventurer who came along. His observations on the perils of mistaking uniformity for unity are very well worth examining, both as a remarkable example of political prophecy and as illustration of the traditional conservative attitude towards the problem of "morbid concentrations of power" in the modern state.

It is boasted that the geometrical policy has been adopted, that all local ideas should be sunk, and that the people should be no longer Gascons, Picards, Bretons, Normans; but Frenchmen, with one country, one heart, and one assembly. But instead of being all Frenchmen, the greater likelihood is that the inhabitants of that region will shortly have no country. No man ever was attached by a sense of pride, partiality, or real affection to a description of square measurements. He never will glory in belonging to the chequer number 71, or to any other badge-ticket. We begin our public affections in our families. No cold relation is a zealous citizen. We pass on to our neighbourhoods, and our habitual provincial connexions. These are inns and resting-places. Such divisions of our country as have been formed by habit, and not by a sudden jerk of authority, were so many little images of the great country in which the heart found something which it could fill. The love to the whole is not extinguished by this subordinate partiality. Perhaps it is a sort of elemental training to those higher and more large regards, by which alone men come to be affected, as with their own concern, in the prosperity of a kingdom. . . . To be attached to the subdivision, to love the little platoon we belong to in society, is the first principle (the germ, as it were) of public affections. It is the first link in the series by which we proceed towards a love of our country, and of mankind.

Classification, if properly ordered, is good in all forms of government; and composes a strong barrier against the excesses of despotism, as well as it is the necessary means of giving effect and permanence to a republic. For want of something of this kind, if the present project of a republic should fail, all securities to a moderated freedom fall along with it; all the indirect restraints which mitigate despotism are removed; insomuch that if monarchy should ever again obtain an entire ascendancy in France, under this or any other dynasty, it will probably be, if not voluntarily tempered, at setting out, by the wise and virtuous counsels of the prince, the most completely arbitrary power that has ever appeared on earth.

(vii) *The Diffusion of Power:* (2) *Disraeli*

Disraeli's treatment of this principle is bound up with his attack on Whiggism. He identified whig government with oligarchy, monopoly, centralisation of power—all the vices which Burke and Coleridge associated with Jacobinism, and which later critics associate with the manifold forms of modern totalitarianism. Disraeli's remedy for the disease was the inculcation of respect for the reality and multiformity of the ancient institutions of the country.

The following passages are taken from *The Spirit of Whiggism* (1834) and *The O'Connell Letters* (1835).

I challenge anyone to quote any speech I have ever made, or one line I have ever written, hostile to the institutions of the country; on the contrary, I have never omitted any opportunity of showing that on the maintenance of those institutions the liberties of the nation depended: that if the Crown, the Church, the House of Lords, the corporations, the magistracy, the poor laws were successfully attacked, we should fall, as once before we nearly fell, under a grinding oligarchy, and inevitably be governed by a metropolis.

The rights and liberties of a nation can only be preserved by institutions. . . . Cultivation of intellect and diffusion of knowledge may make the English nation more sensible of the benefits of their social system, and better qualified to discharge the duties with which their institutions have invested them, but they will never render them competent to preserve their liberties without the aid of these institutions. Let us for a moment endeavour to fancy Whiggism in a state of rampant predominance; let us try to contemplate England enjoying all those advantages which our present rulers have not yet granted us, and some of which they have as yet only ventured to promise by innuendo. Let us suppose our ancient monarchy abolished, our independent hierarchy reduced to a stipendiary sect, the gentlemen of England deprived of their magisterial functions, and metropolitan prefects and sub-prefects established in the counties and principal towns, commanding a vigorous and vigilant police, and backed by an army under the immediate orders of a single House of Parliament. Why, these are threatened changes—ay, and not one of them that may not be brought about to-morrow under the plea of " the spirit of the age " or " county reform " or " cheap government ". But where then will be the liberties of England? Who will dare disobey

London? . . . When these merry times arrive—the times of extraordinary tribunals and extraordinary taxes—and, if we proceed in our present course, they are much nearer than we imagine—the phrase Anti-Reformer will serve as well as that of Malignant, and be as valid a plea as the former title for harassing and plundering all those who venture to wince under the crowning glories of centralisation.

(viii) *The Diffusion of Power:* (3) *Salisbury*

The following excerpt from a speech on Conservative Policy at Newport, Mon., on October 7, 1885, by Lord Salisbury, illustrates the persistence of the Conservative advocacy of a more equitable balance of initiative and authority between central and local government.

Now bear in mind what true reform in Local Government means. It does not only mean—what I quite admit—that the local authorities should be popularly elected; but it means that, when you have got at what you want, when you have provided the proper constitution of local authority, you must provide that the local authority has sufficient powers, and that it gets those powers by diminishing the excessive and exaggerated powers that have been heaped on the central authorities in London. And that I claim to be a special Tory doctrine, which we have held, through good report and evil report, for many and many a generation. It has always been our contention that the people in their localities should govern themselves—and that the attempt to imitate Continental plans by drawing all authority from the central power, though it might produce a more scientific, a more exact, and, for the moment, a more effective administration, yet was destitute of these two essentials of all good government. It did not provide a government that was suited to the facts and idiosyncrasies of the particular community for whom it was designed, and it did not teach the people to take that active interest in their own government which is the only training that makes a man a true and worthy citizen. These are the doctrines that we have held for a very long time. We urged them—that is to say, our fathers urged them—perhaps with undue insistence, when they opposed the introduction of the New Poor Law. It was a necessary reform in order to meet tremendous evils, but one of the results of it is, that this sort of centralisation has eaten far too deeply into our institutions. . . . I feel that the education of the country has so far advanced, that the dissemination of men capable of taking a part in Local Government is so great, that the time has come when many of those powers which are now given to the Local Government Board, and other authorities in London, ought to be given to county authorities, who will be able to govern not necessarily in the most scientific and accurate fashion, but in a fashion which is liked by the people over whom they rule. . . .

(ix) *The Diffusion of Power:* (4) *Quintin Hogg*

From Chapter 10 of *The Case for Conservatism* by Quintin Hogg.

Political liberty is nothing else but the diffusion of power. All power tends to corrupt, absolute power to corrupt absolutely. It follows that political liberty is impossible to the extent that power is concentrated in the hands of a few men. It does not matter whether these be popularly elected or no. Give men power and they will misuse it. Give them absolute power, that is, concentrate in their hands all the various kinds and degrees of power, and they will abuse it absolutely. If power is not to be abused it must be spread as widely as possible throughout the community.

Thus, although Conservatives have always supported a strong central authority when the danger to order has consisted in too much decentralisation, to-day they believe that it would be an evil day for Britain, and for freedom, if all power fell into the hands of the Cabinet. For since political liberty is nothing else than the diffusion of power, the splitting up of political and legal power into different parcels is the essential means of securing it. . . .

Just as political democracy and political freedom means the diffusion, the sharing of political power, so economic democracy, economic freedom, means the sharing, the diffusion, of economic power, that is property, as widely as possible throughout the community. . . .

As Conservatives see it, the whole outlook and philosophy of the Labour Movement can be summed up in the single phrase " Concentration of Power ". No one pretends that the distribution of power is, or ever has been, perfect. It may be, or rather of course it is, the duty of men of good will to subject this distribution to continuous improvement. But Conservatives believe that the deliberate policy of concentrating more and more power in the hands of the executive is to jump from the frying-pan into the fire.

CHAPTER 4

THE FUNCTIONS OF GOVERNMENT

To the Conservative, all the functions of government are limited, or minimum, functions, because government is only one among many of the means by which men pursue their natural and supernatural ends. It is not a God, a grandmother, or a universal provider.

The first function of government is the minimum use of force in the interests of public order and justice. Conservatism accepts the use of force for this limited but essential purpose without fear or prudery.

The second function of government is the administration of justice according to a known body of public law.

The third function is to remove obstacles in the path of individual self-agency and to provide the minimum material requirements of a free and civilised life for all citizens. How far government should go in this last respect, into what fields its actions should penetrate, Conservatives regard as entirely a matter of expediency. They hold steadily and always to one principle: that what men *do* is less important than what men *are*, that the motives on which they act are at least as important as the results of their actions, and that it is better for men to do things voluntarily, on the principle of moral free-agency (which is the only freedom worth anything), than to have certain lines of action imposed on them without the active and intelligent co-operation of their will and convictions. " All reform," Coleridge once wrote, " or innovation not won from the free agent by the presentation of juster views and nobler interests . . . it were folly to propose and worse than folly to attempt."

For the purpose of this active and rational conception of liberty, Conservatives believe that the possession of private property is indispensable.

(i) *The Minimum of Force*

The following terse summary of the Conservative attitude to government as the art of directing public force is taken from Kenneth Pickthorn's essay, *Principles and Prejudices* (Signpost Books, 1943).

Politics is the art of directing public force. In Britain nowadays we can take it for granted that public force is easily stronger than all others put together, that as far as material strength goes, and also as far as legal competence goes, whatever the King in Parliament enacts is the law, and whatever is the law, government has enough agents and instruments, from telephone girls to tanks, to enforce; force is of the essence of the affair.

Nobody likes having force used upon him; anybody who is adult knows that the one thing certain about others is their possession of equal rights with himself, and therefore anyone adult enough for citizenship should dislike using force on others. Any society in which many members were conscious during much of the time of constraint by the force of others would be an uncomfortable society; any society in which there was much conscious pleasure in constraining others would be a wicked society. Therefore, the less compulsion there is in any society, the better; and all the more so as most people believe (even, in Britain, most of those who call themselves Marxists or materialists of some other sort) that there are moral and spiritual values; for, clearly, if there are such values they exceed material values, and, clearly, no act done under compulsion can as such have spiritual value: if you refrain from murder because of the hangman, that is of value to your enemy, but it is much less valuable to you and to society than if your virtue were real, that is, unforced. . . .

To discourage and bluff the State out of the necessary use of force is the sure way to arrive in the end at the *maximum* use of force, the minimum of liberty: when the inhabitants of a state despair of getting order from their existing government, that is the moment when they will turn to anyone—fascist, communist, militarist, royalist, or whatever else—who will promise to enforce authority, so that they shall at least know what to expect. For the ordinary man, not much abler or more fortunate than most other men, the worst of all political ills is the doubt what adventurer or what faction, what armed doctrine or ambitious interest, will next be putting constraint on society or on some section of it. Constraint is every man's enemy, and the price of liberty is eternal vigilance; it is not less true that order is every man's necessity, and that in a society where virtue is not complete and general, the only guarantee of order is that the authority shall have overwhelming force, and enough belief in itself to judge when the use of force is necessary, and then to use it.

(ii) *The Rule of Law*

Conservatism is not singular, among English political creeds, in its devotion to the "Rule of Law". Respect for the rule of law is an ancient English habit. It has, however, been threatened by the growth of the Socialist doctrine of government as the electoral mandate: the notion that whatever a majority of the electorate has supported, or has seemed to support, at a General Election, must be put into legislative operation. In order to counter it, Conservatism emphasises the "Rule of Law". In its simplest form, that counter-attack is open to many criticisms.

For example, the "Rule of Law" is apt to be another name for the "rule of lawyers". In any case, the law may be thoroughly bad. Moreover, uncritical adherence to "the law" on the part of those in possession is always to be suspected. However, it is necessary to state the principles involved, with the caution that they are in no sense the prerogative of Conservatism, and that there is a great deal more to be said on the subject than the rather simple Conservative adherents of the doctrine appear to realise.

The following statement is taken from Chapter 13 of Mr. Quintin Hogg's *The Case for Conservatism* (1947). For further discussion the reader is recommended to consult A. V. Dicey's *The Law of the Constitution* and W. I. Jennings's *The Law and the Constitution.*

The first fundamental principle of the rule of law is that a man can only be punished for doing something already against a public law duly passed at the time it was done, after adequate discussion, applied by the judgement of an impartial court properly set up after a public hearing of the case, and executed by public officers duly appointed for the purpose.

The second fundamental principle of the rule of law is that all, even the most powerful and wealthy, are bound to obey it. . . .

A third fundamental principle of the rule of law is that people should not take the law into their own hands. This rule is not absolute; all civilised codes admit in some degree the principle of self-help or self-defence. But, except in extreme emergencies, the rule of law excludes self-help. . . . This was the fundamental objection which Conservatives had to the General Strike in 1926. . . .

A further principle of the rule of law is that laws should be passed only after adequate and public discussion.

(iii) *Legislative interference and the Principle of Moral Free-Agency*

The moral philosophy which underlies the Conservative attitude towards state intervention can be summed up in the statement that our actions are valuable only in so far as they are informed by our rational will, because only then do they spring from and in turn modify our character. Only when our moral being participates in what we do, can our actions have value for the growth of our moral, spiritual and intellectual being, here or hereafter.

This is the highest ground on which Conservative individualism can base itself, and it deserves to be more widely understood than it is—even among Conservatives.

I. COLERIDGE

Coleridge expressed the principle of moral free-agency, or spiritual voluntarism, in the following excerpt from a letter to a friend in 1809, explaining the principles on which he had grounded his periodical, *The Friend*. It is printed in E. Leslie Griggs's edition of Coleridge's *Unpublished Letters*, Vol. II, pp. 1–3.

I . . . shall deem myself amply remunerated if in consequence of my exertions a few only of those who had formed their moral creed on Hume, Paley and their imitators, with or without a belief in the facts of mere historical Christianity, shall have learnt to value actions primarily as the language and natural effect of the state of the agent; if they shall consider what they *are* instead of what they *do*; so that the fig-tree may bring forth its own fruit from its own living principle, and not have the figs tied on to its barren sprays by the hand of outward prudence and respect of character.

2. LORD EUSTACE PERCY

This excerpt is taken from an essay which Lord Eustace Percy contributed to a volume entitled *The Conservative Attitude and Conservative Social Policy* in 1935, and shows the Coleridgean moral tradition still alive.

[The authority of government] is an authority exercised for moral ends, " for the punishment of evil-doers and the praise of them that do well "; but it is exercised by force, and force, while it can secure the outward observance of the moral law, can never regenerate society. It has become a popular habit in recent years to speak of " the State " as if it were a synonym for the whole range of organised social action, and this confused thinking is one of the greatest dangers of the modern world. The State is compulsion. It is law backed by the sanction of punishment. It is compulsion even if it is only the familiar compulsion of taxation. And nineteen hundred years ago the world was shaken to its foundations and changed for all time by the proclamation of the truth that salvation cannot come by the law. . . .

If the State sets about its task in the belief that . . . material comforts are, indeed, the " essence " of liberty and that freedom of thought and association can be lightly sacrificed to gain them, then such a policy must destroy the secret reserve of spiritual power which, manifested in individual men and in voluntary associations of men, has over and over again throughout history changed and re-made human society, and in which lies the only real hope of human redemption. . . .

Perhaps the most distinctive quality of conservative reform . . . is to be found, not in its aims or in its scope, but in its method. . . . Social reconstruction may well require at this moment an unprecedented exercise of central authority, but the aim of its exercise must be, not to establish a new permanent system of government regulation, but to open a new era of individual emancipation.

(iv) *What the State* CANNOT *do*

Although Burke's attitude to state intervention was governed considerably by the fact that the state in his time had not the *means* of extensive intervention, it will be apparent from the following passage that he had an instinctive faith in extra-political agencies which ought to be trusted to operate favourably to the public welfare and social vigour. The passage is taken from *Thoughts and Details on Scarcity* (1795).

It is one of the finest problems in legislation . . . " what the state ought to take upon itself to direct by the public wisdom, and what it ought to leave, with as little interference as possible, to individual discretion." Nothing, certainly, can be laid down on the subject that will not admit of exceptions, many permanent, some occasional. But the clearest line of distinction I could draw, whilst I had my chalk to draw any line, was this: that the state ought to confine itself to what regards the state, namely the exterior establishment of its religion; its magistracy; its revenue; its military force by land and sea; the corporations that owe their existence to its fiat; in a word, to everything that is *truly and properly public*—to the public peace, to the public safety, to the public order, to the public prosperity. In its preventive policy it ought to be sparing in its efforts, and to employ means, rather few, unfrequent and strong, than many, and frequent—and, of course, as they multiply their puny politic race, and dwindle—small and feeble. Statesmen who know themselves will, with the dignity which belongs to wisdom, proceed only in this, the superior orb . . . whatever remains will, in a manner, provide for itself. But as they descend from the state to a province, from a province to a parish, and from a parish to a private house, they will go on accelerated in their fall. They *cannot* do the

lower duty; and, in proportion as they try it, they will
certainly fail in the higher. They ought to know the
different departments of things; what belongs to laws,
and what manners alone can regulate. To these, great
politicians may give a leaning, but they cannot give a
law. . . .

My opinion is against an over-doing of any sort of
administration, and more especially against this most
momentous of all meddling on the part of authority:
the meddling with the subsistence of the people.

(v) *What the State ought to do*
This passage, from Coleridge's *Second Lay Sermon* (1817), is
notable for its statement of the duties of government as a
"hinderer of hindrances" to freedom, and as a provider of the
minimum conditions of a civilised life for the citizen.

Let us suppose the negative ends of a State already
attained, namely, its own safety by means of its own
strength, and the protection of person and property for
all its members. There will then remain its positive
ends: (1) To make the means of subsistence more easy
to each individual, (2) to secure to each of its members
the hope of bettering his own condition and that of
his children, (3) the development of these faculties
which are essential to his humanity, that is, to his
rational and moral being. Under the last head I do
not mean those degrees of intellectual cultivation which
distinguish man from man in the same civilised society,
but those only that raise the civilised man above the
barbarian, the savage and the brute. I require, however, on the part of the State, on behalf of all its
members, not only the outward means of knowing their
essential duties and dignities as men and free men, but
likewise, and more especially, the discouragement of

all such tenures and relations as must, in the very nature of things, render this knowledge inert and cause the good seed to perish as it falls. Such at least is the appointed aim of a state: and at whatever distance from the ideal mark the existing circumstances of a nation may unhappily place the actual statesman, still every movement ought to be in this direction. But the negative merit of not forwarding—the exemption from the crime of necessitating—the debasement and virtual disfranchisement of any class of the community, may be demanded of every State under all circumstances: and the Government that pleads difficulties in repulse or demur of this claim impeaches its own wisdom and fortitude.

Nothing more can be asked of the State, no other duty imposed on it, than to withhold or retract all extrinsic or artificial aids to an injurious system: or, at the utmost, to invalidate in extreme cases such claims as have arisen indirectly from the letter or unforeseen operations of particular statutes: claims that instead of being contained in the right of its proprietary trustees are encroachments on its own rights, and a destructive trespass on a part of its own inalienable and untransferable property—I mean the health, strength, honesty, and filial love of its children. An injurious system, the connivance at which we scarcely dare more than regret in the Cabinet or Senate of an Empire, may justify an earnest reprobation in the management of private estates: provided always that the system only be denounced and the pleadings confined to the court of conscience.[1] For from this court only can the redress be awarded. All reform or innovation not won from the free agent by the presentation of juster views and

---

[1] Cf. Part II, Chapter 6, Section viii, below.

nobler interests, and which does not leave the merit of having effected it sacred to the individual proprietor, it were folly to propose and worse than folly to attempt.

(vii) *State intervention: the Conservative position summed up*

The best summary of the Conservative position in this matter is undoubtedly that afforded by Lord Hugh Cecil in his book *Conservativism* (1912), Chapter VI.

In many respects . . . the individual is as much derived from the State as the State is from the individual. His health and strength, his mental outlook, even so much of his character as depends on environment, have been largely affected by what the State has done. But there is a centre of spiritual life in human nature which lies beyond the sphere of the State. And this life has sometimes power to be independent of all surrounding conditions. Almost everything in the mind and body have been modified by civilization; but examples of human virtue and sanctity are to be found in circumstances untouched by the hand of the State. . . . This is only an illustration . . . that the spiritual life of the Christian is essentially spiritual, and that, though it expresses itself in political and social action, it exists and is subject to the power of grace only within the individual soul. When, therefore, we are judging, as we are bound to do, political action by a moral standard, the State has to conform to the individual's code. . . .

And the principle that the action of the State must be judged by the canons of morality which apply to individuals will carry us further. It follows that the State, no more than any individual in the State, may inflict injustice on anyone. . . . The State as a trustee acting for others may, and indeed must, prefer the good of the community to the good of any individual or minority. But it may not, any more than an honest trustee, inflict injustice in the interest of those for whom it acts. . . . To punish the innocent in the interest of the community is immoral and cannot be justified. And if the State may not punish an innocent man, neither may it inflict upon such a man what is in reality a punishment by disguising it under another name. A pecuniary fine does not cease to be an injustice because it is called a tax or a readjustment of property. It is an injury; and the principle by which the State must be guided is the simple one that it is immoral to inflict an injury upon an innocent man. When, therefore, it is said that the State must act for the common good, that proposition must be subject to the reservation that State action must not in any case be immoral, and that to injure innocent people is immoral. . . . The State must seek the good of the whole community and the good of every individual who is a member of it, but subject to the condition that it must never be guilty of the injustice of inflicting an injury, unless as the punishment of a crime. . . .

For the State to intervene directly to regulate the amount of wealth which an individual may be permitted to acquire seems to involve injustice and to be in itself unwise; but the State has interfered, and is often urged to interfere further, in the mechanism of trade and industry, not with a view of controlling the acquisitions of individuals, but in the general interest of the whole community. With this purpose elaborate laws have been passed to avoid accidents in mining and other dangerous occupations, to regulate factories and workshops in the interest of the public health, to

85

limit or altogether to prohibit the employment of children and, less rigorously, of women. Quite recently measures have been taken to protect miners, although adult men, from what are thought to be excessive hours of labour, and to require, in respect of certain sweated trades, that the wages paid should be subject to the control of a wages board. Broadly speaking, these interventions of the State are defended on two principles. First, that the result that they have achieved is a desirable one; and secondly, that owing to the circumstances of the particular case they cannot be attained by the voluntary action of the persons directly concerned. These reasons seem sound. But there is an ambiguity in them which conceals a latent danger. What is meant by a desirable object? A law may be thought desirable by a government which is, in fact, not thought desirable by the workmen whose industry it regulates. Or it may be thought desirable by some of the workmen concerned, but not by all. . . . It is plain that legislation might become very oppressive if the State is to intervene not only to protect persons who cannot protect themselves, which is the case with women and children, and may be the case in some employments with men also, but to enforce upon adult human beings perfectly able to judge of their own interests, a particular way of following their occupation. A second danger is that, while it is sometimes true that poor men cannot protect themselves in making bargains with rich men, it must not be assumed without careful reflection that no voluntary way of protecting themselves exists, and that they are obliged to have recourse to the power of the State. It may often happen that by combination or otherwise workmen may find their own way out of an inequality in bargaining, and may be able to do without the help of the State. It is far better if such a way can be found, because the State in the end depends on the vigour of the character of the individuals which make it up: and that character is strengthened by the effort to find a way out of difficulties and hardships, and is weakened by the habit of looking to State help. Probably if the ideas that are now dominant had equally prevailed sixty years ago, the State would have done for workmen what trade unions and collective bargaining have done. The difference would certainly not have been to the advantage of the workmen. A trade union is in the workmen's own control and is a flexible organisation which can be adapted from time to time as need requires. The State is controlled by a complexity of forces certainly not identical with the desires of a workman in a particular trade. And the State is a clumsy, rigid instrument difficult to handle and operating heavily and unexpectedly. It might easily have happened that workmen would have found themselves in a position unpleasantly approximating to State slavery, governed at every turn by bureaucratic regulations and, worst of all, enervated by having all the conditions of their industry ordered for them and nothing left to their own initiative and resolution. . . .

But it is a still graver objection to State action that it has none of the educative side of a voluntary effort. Workmen combining together in a trade union to get better wages or shorter hours obtain not only the wages or the hours for which they strive, but a most valuable social and political education by the way. They have to learn to work with one another; they have to learn to respect public opinion; they have to learn to be reasonably regardful of the interests of other

87

persons. The very fact that trade unions have often done unwise things is the best testimony to their real value; for it is only by doing unwise things, or at least having the opportunity to do them, that human beings can ever effectually learn wisdom.

But I do wrong in enlarging on this topic, for, as long as State action does not involve what is unjust or oppressive, it cannot be said that the principles of Conservatism are hostile to it. . . . The questions that arise as to the respective spheres of the State and the individual cannot, in short, be answered by Conservatives with any general answer. The only proposition of a general character that can be laid down is that the State must not treat individuals unjustly, that is, must not inflict upon them undeserved injury. This condition granted, any scheme for enlarging the function of the State must be judged by Conservatives merely on its merits without reference to any general formula, but from a standpoint prudently distrustful of the untried, and preferring to develop what exists rather than to demolish and reconstruct. Conservative social reform need not, therefore, proceed on purely individualist lines. There is no antithesis between Conservatism and Socialism, or even between Conservatism and Liberalism. Subject to the counsels of prudence and a preference for what exists and has been tried over the unknown, Conservatives have no difficulty in welcoming the social activity of the State. The point which principally distinguishes their attitude from that of other political parties is a rigorous adherence to justice. This involves resistance to any measure which would impoverish classes or individuals by depriving them of all or even of a considerable fraction of what they possess. It is so plain that to take what one man has and give it to another is unjust, even though the first man be rich and the second man poor, that it is surprising that legislative measures which consist essentially in such transfers should ever be advocated or defended. . . .

Conservatives thus support measures of social reform as cordially as any political school, but more scrupulously than some. The object of such reforming legislation is, of course, not in any sense a matter of controversy between the Conservative and other parties. All are agreed in the desire to mitigate suffering. To the Conservative this purpose comes with a sacred sanction, for the religious foundation of his Tory beliefs gives to the sorrows of the poor an urgent claim upon his care. But the same religious convictions which inculcate sympathy for suffering teach also the supreme authority of justice; and it is in insisting that injustice shall not stain national help to the afflicted that Conservatism finds in respect to social reform its peculiar and distinctive task.

(vii) *Property as affording " a sphere of individual free-agency "*

To the Conservative, the political importance of private property is that it affords to the individual a sphere of free-agency *vis-à-vis* the state. Where the principle of the sanctity of private property is respected, the individual has literally a " standing " upon which to base his power of personal decision and choice, or a " sphere " within which he can—without anti-social intention —exercise those powers and faculties of a free man.

Coleridge, the moral philosopher of Conservatism, expressed this conception of private property throughout his political writings. In one place, at least, he went so far as to assert that government and law should only take account of persons as exponents of property. This passage occurs in a letter he wrote to Daniel Stuart, October 30, 1814 (*The Letters of S. T. Coleridge*, ed. by E. H. Coleridge, pp. 634–639).

Human jurisprudence, wisely aware of its own weakness, and sensible how incommensurate its powers are with so vast an object as the well-being of individuals, as individuals . . . knows nothing of persons other than as properties, officiaries, subjects. . . . The law knows nothing about guilt. . . . The pretence of considering persons not states, happiness not property, always has ended, and always will end, in making a new STATE or corporation, infinitely more oppressive than the former; and in which the real freedom of persons is as much less, as the things interfered with are more numerous and more minute.

(viii) *Property and Liberty*

The growth of Socialism, and the consequent concentration of power in the State, or in central authority, has led Conservatives to take up once more the argument that property is an essential safeguard of liberty. The following passage from Kenneth Pickthorn's *Principles and Prejudices* (1943) illustrates this return to a basic element in the Conservative tradition.

Almost all our ancestors for a very long time, and till a very recent period, were quite certain that upon property reposed not only all hope of prosperity but also all assurance of liberty. They were so sure of this that on the axiom that every Englishman inherited a right to the law's protection of his goods they founded arguments for his right to dispose of his own person, to freedom of movement, personal liberty. This deducing of liberty from property may seem nowadays to many like hanging a house from its roof. But those who think that there can be no liberty without economic revolution, who want to abolish property in order to multiply freedom, may reasonably be reminded that historically almost all they revere as a striving for liberties was a striving also for property. They may be reminded also that no one has as yet explained how, when Government owns and manages all material goods, the Individual will retain any freedom of movement and discussion. At any rate they will not be able to deny that Property exists. . . . The Conservative will approach property as a conception which has been useful for centuries, which is almost indispensable to our thinking now, which has been and is abused, which has been and must be continually modified, which is in no particular above question, but whose total destruction must cause misery and might cause little else. . . . Against the assumption that there can be no personal or political freedom without economic equality we will contrast the memory that for centuries Englishmen felt themselves freer than other men, and that there has been no liberty except where there has been property.

(ix) *A Rationale of Property*

The following passages from Mr. Quintin Hogg's *The Case for Conservatism* (1947) afford a summary of the Conservative attitude towards private property.

The institution of private property is to be justified on four main interconnected grounds.

First, the possession of private property is a right of the individual—a legitimate aspiration which human beings as such are naturally entitled to pursue as a means of developing their personalities.

Second, private property is the natural right and safeguard of the family, which is itself the natural unit of society and is and ought to be the foundation of the whole fabric of civilized society.

Third, private property is to the interest of the community since the desire to obtain it provides an incentive for work which is morally legitimate, and at the same time sufficiently material to operate on natures which in most of us contain certain elements not entirely spiritual or unselfseeking.

Fourth, private property — including some large fortunes—is the natural bulwark of liberty because it ensures that economic power is not entirely in the hands of the State. . . .

The possession of property by the individual is the essential condition of this liberty. No man is fully free unless possessing some rights of property in something, since property is the means whereby he develops his personality by impressing it upon his external surroundings without dependence on the will of others. No degree of security, no ration scale however generous, no organized hostelry with furniture and services all provided, no uniform clothing however lavish or becoming is a substitute for property. Property is in itself a good and a legitimate aspiration for human striving.

When property is achieved, it becomes a responsibility —a duty as well as a right—a duty to develop the property as a thing of beauty or utility for the honour of God, a duty to share it with others as a means of winning their love and understanding, a duty to use it in such a way that it does not infringe the human rights and dignities of others. . . .

According to Conservatives, the aim of every man may legitimately include the possession of enough private property to own, if he desires it, a house and a garden, to bring up a family including the provision of a slightly better education than the table d'hote afforded by the State, to indulge a reasonable hobby or leisure time occupation, and to end in his old age with a little more than the State pension, however generous. These are his aims, and he should be given not the realisation of them, but a fair chance in life to realise them. . . .

Secondly, private property is a natural right of the family, and generally of the subordinate group. . . . Conservatives . . . refuse to treat either the State or the individual as absolute. Human souls, as they see it, exist as individuals, but as individuals forming part not merely of a political community but of various groups, of which the most important is the family. The perpetuation of these groups — families, local communities, voluntary associations—is a prime object of Conservative policy; Conservatives also regard it as essential to their perpetuation that groups and individuals should be able to possess and bequeath private property, including, if need be, considerable fortunes.

In particular, although Conservatives are prepared to concede the necessity of a graduated death duty as a means of keeping wealth fairly distributed, they are unable to understand the idea that men should be entitled to make fortunes for themselves but not be free to bequeath them to others when they die. They are convinced that to deprive them of this is to deprive them of one of the rights to which human beings are properly entitled as such to aspire. . . .

Conservatives believe that the incentive to possess property by legitimate means is one of the most valuable aids to the production and increase of wealth. Provided that others are not thereby impoverished or harmed they consider that the possession of large fortunes is a good—a good both absolutely and relatively because it tends to the diffusion of economic power and away from its concentration in the hands of the Government. Nor have Conservatives the smallest objection to the existence of a leisured class which uses its leisure well. On the contrary, however short the working hours of life become, Conservatives believe that a leisured class has much to bring to society—both in culture and wisdom. . . .

Two qualifications need to be made of the general position that Conservatives defend and support the institution of private property.

In the first place the fact that Conservatives defend property as an institution does not mean that they necessarily defend any particular kind or sort of property. For instance, more Conservatives than myself do not approve of a situation in which a great portion of the ground rents of Cardiff are owned by a limited company in London, and do not believe that a little line of working-class houses is a suitable investment for the life-savings of a capitalist. . . .

But, secondly, there are also cases where the rights of private owners, although themselves perfectly legitimate, ought not to prevail against the public interest.[1] The clearest example is the generally conceded right of the government to acquire land for public purposes. Both Acquisition of Land Acts and Housing Acts provide examples of this kind.

Nevertheless in both these cases—both where a right is acquired or when one is extinguished — however undesirable, Conservatives believe that proper compensation should be paid.

For these reasons Conservatives maintain that wherever it is legitimate—and for whatever reasons—to

---

[1] " Every Canal Bill proves that there is no species of property which the legislature does not possess and exercise right of controlling and limiting, as soon as the right of the individuals is shown to be disproportionately injurious to the community." Coleridge, *Two Addresses on Sir Robert Peel's Bill* (1818). Legislative intervention to control or extinguish private rights in the common interest, as a principle within the Conservative tradition, is dealt with in Chapter 4, Section III, above.

override the proprietary rights of the individual it is the business of the state to provide sufficient compensation to safeguard the legitimate expectations of those who are expropriated.

CHAPTER 5

THE STATE IN RELATION TO THE CHURCH

Respect for, and defence of, religion is no monopoly of the Conservative tradition. The Conservative tradition at its best, however, does avow steadily and intelligently the primacy of religion in human affairs, its indispensability to any adequate account of social cohesion among civilised peoples, and its sovereign power as a criticism and a check upon secular governments—the ambition of personal rulers, or the never-ending audacity of elected persons.

(i) *Burke*

In his *Reflections on the Revolution in France* (1790), Burke was not only defending the ecclesiastical institutions of his country, but was upholding the religious view of politics and government against the mechanical materialism which had found expression in the overthrow of the Church in France. Here we have perhaps the best expression of his view that an established religion makes for a proper humility on the part of secular power and a healthy respect for the long-term interests of society—the permanent part of man's nature. This, Burke held, is especially important in a democracy, which needs, even more than a monarchy or an aristocracy, to be constantly reminded that its will is not the standard of right and wrong [see Chapter 3, section (i)]. He would uphold the civic value of an ecclesiastical establishment as an independent power in the state in order that its criticism of secular authority may be a real one. To those who would hold that the Church is a mere ally of a ruling class "to keep the vulgar in obedience", he would reply: first, that it is not easy for a class to make others believe in a moral system to which that class itself gives no credit; and secondly, that the rich and powerful need the instruction and consolation of religion even more than do the poor.

[The consecration of the state by a religious establishment] is made that all who administer in the government of men . . . should have high and worthy notions of their function and destination; that their hope should be full of immortality; that they should not look to the paltry pelf of the moment . . . but to a solid, permanent existence, in the permanent part of their nature, and to a permanent fame and glory in the example they leave as a rich inheritance to the world.

Such sublime principles ought to be infused into persons of exalted situations; and religious establishments provided that may continually revive and enforce them. . . . The consecration of the state by a state religious establishment is necessary also to operate with a wholesome awe upon free citizens. . . . All persons possessing any portion of power ought to be strongly and awfully impressed with an idea that they act in trust; and that they are to account for their conduct in that trust to the one great Master, Author and Founder of society. This principle ought even to be more strongly impressed upon the minds of those who compose the collective sovereignty than upon those of single princes. . . . It is . . . of infinite importance that they should not be suffered to imagine that their will, any more than that of kings, is the standard of right and wrong. They ought to be persuaded that they are full as little entitled, and far less qualified with safety to themselves, to use any arbitrary power whatsoever. . . .

It is on some such principles that the majority of the people of England, far from thinking a religious national establishment unlawful, hardly think it lawful to be without one. . . . They do not consider their church establishment as convenient, but as essential to their state; not as a thing heterogeneous and separable; something added for accommodation; that they may either keep or lay aside, according to their temporary ideas of convenience. They consider it as the foundation of their whole constitution, with which, and with every part of which, it holds an indissoluble union. Church and state are ideas inseparable in their minds, and scarcely is the one ever mentioned without mentioning the other. . . .

It is from our attachment to a church establishment, that the English nation did not think it wise to entrust that great, fundamental interest of the whole . . . to the unsteady and precarious contribution of individuals. . . . The people of England think that they have constitutional motives, as well as religious, against any project of turning their independent clergy into ecclesiastical pensioners of state. . . . They therefore made their church, like their kings and their nobility, independent. From the united considerations of religion and constitutional policy, from their opinion of a duty to make a sure provision for the consolation of the feeble and the instruction of the ignorant, they have incorporated and identified the estate of the church with the mass of *private property*, of which the state is not the proprietor, either for use or dominion, but the guardian only and the regulator. They have ordained that the provision of this establishment might be as stable as the earth on which it stands, and should not fluctuate with the Euripus of funds and actions. . . .

If by their conduct (the only language that rarely lies) they seemed to regard the great ruling principle

of the moral and the natural world as a mere invention
to keep the vulgar in obedience, they apprehend that
by such a conduct they would defeat the politic purpose
they have in view. They would find it difficult to make
others believe in a system to which they manifestly gave
no credit themselves. The Christian statesmen of this
land would, indeed, first provide for the *multitude*;
because it is the *multitude*; and is therefore, as such,
the first object in the ecclesiastical institution, and in all
institutions. . . . But as they know that charity is not
confined to any one description, but ought to apply
itself to all men who have wants, they are not deprived
of a due and anxious sensation of pity to the distresses
of the miserable great. . . .

(ii) *The National Church and the National Culture*

Coleridge was a disciple of Burke, and in his *On the Constitution of the Church and State, according to the Idea of Each*
(1830) he worked out a theory of religion and the Church in
relation to the Body Politic which Gladstone described as " alike
beautiful and profound ". Coleridge argues that since a healthy
State, or Society, depends upon the acceptance and maintenance
of a true philosophy, it must accept and maintain a National
Church as guardian and teacher of that philosophy through
the vehicle of a philosophically-based religion. Without this, a
Nation can be neither permanent nor progressive. The purposes
of the National Church, to Coleridge, are: to guard, improve
and inculcate the national culture, and to produce thereby a
citizenry properly grounded in its rights and duties. The Church
has thus a properly political function on the highest of all
grounds: to put men in the way of realising their finest potentialities within the framework of the State. The following
passages are taken from *The Constitution of the Church and
State*, Chapters 5 and 6.

There remains for the third estate [the estate of the
Church] only that interest which is the ground, the

necessary antecedent condition, of both the former [i.e. the estates of Permanence and Progression]. But civilisation is itself but a mixed good . . . and the nation so distinguished more fitly to be called a varnished than a polished people where this civilisation is not grounded in *cultivation*, in the harmonious development of those qualities and faculties that characterise our *humanity*. We must be men in order to be citizens. . . .

The proper object and end of the National Church is civilisation with freedom; and the duty of its ministers . . . would be fulfilled in the communication of that degree and kind of knowledge to all, the possession of which is necessary for all in order to their CIVILITY. By civility I mean all the qualities essential to a citizen, and devoid of which no people or class of the people can be calculated upon by the rulers and leaders of the state for the conservation or promotion of its essential interests. It follows, therefore, that in regard of the grounds and principles of action and conduct, the State has a right to demand of the National Church that its instructions should be fitted to diffuse throughout the people *legality*, that is, the obligations of a well-calculated self-interest under the conditions of a common interest determined by common laws . . . to diffuse throughout the whole community, and to every native entitled to its laws and rights, that quantity and quality of knowledge which was indispensable both for the understanding of those rights and for the performance of the duties correspondent. . . . The object of the two former estates of the realm, which conjointly form the State, was to reconcile the interests of permanence with those of progression— law with liberty. The object of the National Church, the third remaining estate of the realm, was to secure and improve that civilisation without which the nation could be neither permanent nor progressive. . . .

THE CLERISY of the nation, or national church, in its primary acceptation and original intention, comprehended the learned of all denominations;—the sages and professors of the law and jurisprudence; of medicine and physiology; of music; of military and civil architecture; of the physical sciences; with the mathematical as the common organ of the preceding; in short, all the so-called liberal arts and sciences, the possession and application of which constitute the civilisation of a country, as well as the Theological. The last was, indeed, placed at the head of all; and of good right did it claim the precedence. . . . It had the precedency because under the name theology were comprised all the main aids, instruments, and materials of NATIONAL EDUCATION, the *nisis formativus* of the body politic, the shaping and informing spirit, which, *educing*, i.e. eliciting, the latent *man* in all the natives of the soil, *trains them up* to be citizens of the country, free subjects of the realm. And lastly, because to divinity belong those fundamental truths which are the common groundwork of our civil and religious duties, not less indispensable to a right view of our temporal concerns than to a rational faith respecting our immortal well-being. (Not without celestial observations can even terrestrial charts be accurately constructed.) And of special importance is it to the objects here contemplated that, only by the vital warmth diffused by these truths throughout the MANY, and by the guiding light from the philosophy, which is the basis of *divinity*, possessed by the FEW, can either the community or its rulers fully comprehend, or rightly appreciate, the permanent *distinction*, and the occasional *contrast*, between cultivation and civilisation; or be made to understand the most valuable of the lessons taught by history, and exemplified alike in her oldest and her most recent records,—that a nation can never be a too cultivated, but may easily become an over-civilised race.

It is folly to think of making all, or the many, philosophers, or even men of science and systematic knowledge. But it is duty and wisdom to aim at making as many as possible soberly and steadily religious;—in as much as the morality which the state requires in its citizens for its own well-being and ideal immortality, and without reference to their spiritual interest as individuals, can only exist for the people in the form of religion. . . . In fine, Religion, true or false, is and ever has been the centre of gravity in a realm, to which all other things must and will accommodate themselves.

(iii) *Gladstone on the State in its Relation to the Church*

Gladstone, the ardent young Tory, published his book on *The State in its relations with the Church* in 1838. In it, he carries on the Burke tradition of the consecration of the State, as a collective person, and in its agents and members as individuals, by a public and formal acknowledgement of religion. " The principle of an established religion is a natural and legitimate consequence of the mere fact of government," he held. There is the same stress upon political power as a divine trust and upon the negation of mere *will*, whether it be the will of a prince or a people, as constituting law. On the whole, Gladstone lays less emphasis than Coleridge upon the National Church as the organ and the proponent of the national culture, although he fully appreciated the greatness of the conception. In fact, Gladstone's work is the last great exposition of the " Church-State " concept as it was handed down in the tradition of Hooker. An admirable discussion of its meaning and relevance is to be found in Alec Vidler's work, *The Orb and the Cross*.

The style of Gladstone's book is often both flocculent and turbid. The following passages have been selected for their comparative clarity and should give a fair idea of the conception in its principal aspects. Conservatism owes more, in this matter of its teaching with regard to Church and State, to the future leader of the Liberal Party than to any formally Conservative thinker of the nineteenth century.

That in national societies of men generally, the governing body should, in its capacity as such, profess and maintain a religion according to its conscience, both as being composed of individuals who have individual responsibilities to discharge and individual purposes to fulfil, and as being itself, collectively, the seat of a national personality, with national responsibilities to discharge and national purposes to fulfil: that it must have the extrinsic, and, in proportion as it is a good government, will have the intrinsic, qualifications for professing and maintaining such religion: that religion offers sufficient inducements to such a policy: that as, in respect of its extension, it should, for the benefit of the state, be the greatest *possible*, and we are therefore bound to show, in considering the above-mentioned national purposes, that the direct aid of the state promotes that extension: so, in respect of its quality, it should be the *purest* possible, that is to say, should be the Catholic Church of Christ: that such adoption by the state follows in the way of natural order upon the general prevalence of a religion in the community: that the means should be appropriate, and such as are authorised by the rules both of the religion and of the constitution. . . .

While on Christian principles we are commanded to discharge our social duties " as unto the Lord " and not to man, so, even in the view of rationalism, we must ever bear in mind that, whatever be the functions, whatever the external circumstances, of each particular person, he has a nature and a law within him, which protest against being absorbed and lost in the external energies required by those functions; which claim to rule over him and to direct the paramount conditions of his life; and by the supercession of which he surrenders his human birthright and patrimony, the inward and central freedom of his being, and becomes but as a captive, chained, though it may be to a triumphal car. . . .

In fulfilment, then, of his obligations as an individual, the statesman must be a worshipping man. But his acts are public; the powers and instruments with which he works are public: acting under and by the authority of the law, he moves at his word ten thousand subject arms; and, because such energies are thus essentially public and wholly out of the range of mere individual agency, they must be sanctified not only by the private personal prayers and piety of those who fill public situations, but also by public acts of the men composing the public body. They must offer prayer and praise in their public and collective character, in that character wherein they constitute the organ of the nation, and wield its collected force. . . .

Wherever there is power in the universe, that power is the property of God, the king of that universe—his property of right, however for a time withholden or abused. Now this property is as it were realised, is used according to the will of the owner, when it is used for the purpose he has ordained, and in the temper of mercy, justice, truth and faith, which he has taught us. But those principles never can be truly, never can be permanently, entertained in the human breast, except by a continual reference to their source, and the supply of Divine grace. The powers, therefore, that dwell in individuals acting as a government, as well as those that dwell in individuals acting for themselves, can only be secured for right uses by applying to them a religion. . . . The principle of an established religion is a natural and legitimate consequence of the mere fact of government, however defective the idea of religion entertained by the governors. . . .

Political power . . . is equally the property of God; men are equally bound to sanctify it, whether it be derived to the governors immediately or through the people. Where the government is democratic, and the majority are of a given religion, the principle above stated will apply. Where government is founded on paternal principles, and the fiction of popular sovereignty is discountenanced, there the function of choice in the legislature is still more apparent. The latter case is that of our own country. But if there be those who would class it with the former, still the national estate of religion (for we are not yet concerned with it as the church) represents in its present form the religion of the majority of the people, and it is their duty to sustain it in its position. . . .

There is also a real and not merely supposititious personality of nations, which entails likewise its own religious responsibilities. The plainest exposition of national personality is this—that the nation fulfils the great conditions of a person: namely, that it has unity of acting, and unity of suffering; with the difference that what is physically single in the one, is joint, or morally single, in the other. . . . A nation, then, having a personality, lies under the obligation, like the individuals composing its governing body, of sanctifying acts of that personality by the offices of religion, and thus we have a new and imperative ground for the existence of a state religion. . . .

Religion is the great instrument of *making* man—of forming, moulding, educating him. In spite of his natural aversion to things divine, the religion of a country is ever found by experience to have a greater influence on its character and destinies than any other cause. . . . Still more specifically may it be shown how Christian religion contributes to make good subjects; it is by destroying that law of self-will and self-worship, the ancient idol, the great lie of the world, which galls and scourges us even until now. The antagonist truth is, that our mere will does not constitute a rightful law of action, but is always to be led by regard to extrinsic grounds of duty. . . . It is by teaching man not only his actual poverty, but his moral and essential dependence; by teaching him that the mere fact of his wishing to do this or that does not constitute a reason for doing it, unless he can trace that wish up to some higher cause or object; that religion takes away the grand principle, as of individual, so likewise of social misery and disorder. Undoubtedly she does not propose to private persons the will of governors as constituting in all cases a law to which they are implicitly to submit; this were to substitute one human idol for another. But she does this: she inculcates absolute obedience to all law not sinful, while it continues to be law, as the essential condition of order in societies. And with respect to the alteration of laws, or the introduction of new ones, she puts every individual in a condition to exercise with content the functions which the constitution assigns to him . . . she commands one and all concerned to abjure the law of private inclination, and to direct their observation to the common reason and justice of the case. . . .

(iv) *Disraeli on the Church*

Disraeli was at times an embarrassing and suspect champion of the Established Church. An Anglicised Jew, an habitual communicant of the Church of England, he never quite succeeded in convincing his Conservative colleagues and followers as an advocate of the National Church. He clung to it as a national, historic, traditional institution. The Church was a national corporation, not a clerical corporation, and every possible measure should be taken to keep it so. "There are few great things left," he once said, "and the Church is one." The Church was an organ of centrality. It was coincident with the State.

The following passage is taken from a speech at Aylesbury in 1861.

The most powerful principle which governs man is the religious principle. . . . A wise government, allying itself with religion, would as it were consecrate society and sanctify the state. But how is this to be done? It is the problem of modern politics which has always most embarrassed statesmen. No solution of the difficulty is to be found in salaried priesthoods and complicated concordats. But by the side of the state in England there has gradually arisen a majestic corporation—wealthy, powerful, independent,—with the sanctity of a long tradition, yet sympathising with authority, and full of conciliation, even deference, to the civil power. Broadly and deeply planted in the land, mixed up with all our manners and customs, one of the main guarantees of our local government, and therefore one of the prime securities of our common liberties, the Church of England is part of our history, part of our life, part of England itself.

It is said sometimes that the Church of England is hostile to religious liberty. As well might it be said that the monarchy of England is adverse to political freedom. Both are institutions which insure liberty by securing order.

(v) *The New Superstition*

The following passages are taken from an address delivered by Disraeli in the Sheldonian Theatre, Oxford, on November 25, 1864.

Why, my Lord, man is a being born to believe. And if no Church comes forward with its title-deeds of truth, sustained by the tradition of sacred ages and by the conviction of countless generations, to guide him, he will find altars and idols in his own heart and his own imagination. But observe this. What must be the relations of a powerful Church, without distinctive creeds, with a being of such a nature? Why, of course, the chief principle of political economy will be observed. Where there is a great demand there will be a proportionate supply: and commencing, as the new school may, by rejecting the principle of inspiration, it will end by every priest becoming a prophet; and beginning, as they do, by repudiating the practice of miracles, before long, rest assured, we shall be living in a flitting scene of spiritual phantasmagoria. There are no tenets, however extravagant, and no practices, however objectionable, which will not in time develop under such a state of affairs; opinions the most absurd and ceremonies the most revolting. . . . A Church without a distinctive creed will lead, I believe, to a dissoluteness of manners and of morals rarely equalled in the history of man, but which prepares the tomb of empires. . . . Upon our acceptance of that Divine interpretation for which we are indebted to the Church, and of which the Church is the guardian, all sound and salutary legislation depends. That truth is the only security for civilisation, and the only guarantee of real progress.

(vi) *Conservatism and the Establishment*
The Conservative case for the maintenance of the present legal and constitutional relationship between Church and State is stated with perfect clarity and rigorous logic in Chapter 4 of Lord Hugh Cecil's *Conservatism* (1912). There is only space here to give Lord Cecil's conclusions: the text should be consulted in full.

Defence of the Church against attack, either on its established position or on its endowments, is an essential part of the work of Conservatism. Heir of Toryism as it is, it stands for the Church and for the formal recognition of religion by the State. . . .

Conservatives . . . resist Disestablishment and Disendowment. The recognition of religion implied in establishment and the defence of the endowments against confiscation are essential parts of Conservatism, characteristics of the typical Conservative reverence for religion and for property. . . .

Conservatism insists on the national acceptance of Christianity, and desires to reconcile that acceptance with complete toleration of all sorts of opinions on religious matters. . . . Impartiality between religious bodies is not to be achieved by attempting a compromise based on eliminating the more controversial parts of various religious systems and amalgamating the residuum, but by extending an equal measure of assistance and countenance to all sorts of religious opinion. . . .

The championship of religion . . . is the most important of the functions of Conservatism. It is the keystone of the arch upon which the whole fabric rests. As long as Conservatism makes the fulfilment of its duties to religion the first of its purposes, it will be saved from the two principal dangers that alternatively threaten it: the danger of sinking into a mere factious variation of Liberalism, and the danger of standing for the defence of those who are well off. . . . Religion is the standard by which the plans of politicians must be judged, and a religious purpose must purify their aims and methods. Emphasising this truth, Conservatism will be the creed neither of a superfluous faction nor of a selfish class.

(vii) *The Idea of a Christian Society*

Mr. T. S. Eliot's work under the above title yields to the Conservative a number of ideas well within the tradition. although it is the work of a philosophic poet rather than of a typical Conservative publicist. Making allowance for the facts of historical development, Mr. Eliot's thesis bears a remarkable resemblance to that of Coleridge.

The battles over Church Rates, Endowments, and (one hopes) Disestablishment are over, but the battle for a culture based on Christian values is at its crisis, and if Conservatism is alive to its philosophical ancestry and intellectual responsibilities it will see in Mr. Eliot's work its finest armament.

A relation between Church and State . . . implies that the state is in some sense Christian. It must be clear that I do not mean by a Christian State one in which the rulers are chosen because of their qualifications, still less their eminence as Christians. . . . It is not primarily the Christianity of the statesmen that matters, but their being confined, by the temper and traditions of the people which they rule, to a Christian framework within which to realise their ambitions and advance the prosperity and prestige of their country. They may frequently perform un-Christian acts; they must never attempt to defend their actions on un-Christian principles. . . . Among the men of state, you would have as a minimum, conscious conformity of behaviour. In the Christian community that they ruled, the Christian faith would be ingrained, but it requires as a minimum, only a largely unconscious behaviour; and it is only from the much smaller number of conscious human beings, the Community of Christians, that one would expect a conscious Christian life on its highest social level. . . . The rulers, I have said, will, *qua* rulers, accept Christianity not simply as their own faith to guide their actions, but as the system under which they are to govern. The people will accept it as a matter of behaviour and habit. . . .

You cannot expect continuity and coherence in politics, you cannot expect reliable behaviour on fixed principles persisting through changed situations, unless there is an underlying political philosophy: not of a party, but of the nation. You cannot expect continuity and coherence in literature and the arts, unless you have a certain uniformity of culture, expressed in education by a settled, though not rigid agreement as to what everyone should know to some degree, and a positive distinction—however undemocratic it may sound—between the educated and the uneducated. . . . The Community of Christians is not an organisation, but a body of indefinite outline; composed both of clergy and laity, of the more conscious, more spiritually and intellectually developed of both. It will be their identity of belief and aspiration, their background of a common system of education and a common culture, which will enable them to influence and be influenced by each other, and collectively to form the conscious mind and the conscience of the nation. . . .

. . . If the desirability of unity be admitted, if the idea of a Christian society be grasped and accepted, then it can only be realised, in England, through the Church of England. . . . It is this Church which, by reason of its tradition, its organisation, and its relation in the past to the religious-social life of the people, is the one for our purpose. . . . No Christianisation of England can take place without it. . . . The national faith must have an official recognition by the State, as well as an accepted status in the community and a basis of conviction in the heart of the individual. . . .

The danger of a National Church becoming a class Church is not one that concerns us immediately to-day; for now that it is possible to be respectable without being a member of the Church of England, or a Christian of any kind, it is also possible to be a member of the Church of England without being—in that sense—respectable. The danger that a National Church might become also a Nationalistic Church is one to which our predecessors theorising about Church and State could hardly have been expected to devote attention, since the danger of nationalism itself, and the danger of the supersession of every form of Christianity, could not have been very present to their minds . . . I think that the dangers to which a National Church is exposed, when the Universal Church is no more than a pious ideal, are so obvious that only to mention them is to command assent. Completely identified with a particular people, the National Church may at all times, but especially at moments of excitement, become no more than the voice of that people's prejudice, passion or interest. But there is another danger, not quite so easily identified. I have maintained that the idea of a Christian society implies, for me, the existence of one Church which shall *aim at* comprehending the whole nation. Unless it has this aim, we relapse into that conflict between citizenship and churchmembership, between public and private morality, which to-day makes moral life so difficult for everyone, and which in turn provokes that craving for a simplified, monistic solution of statism or racism which the National Church can only combat if it recognises its position as a part of the Universal Church. . . . Even in a Christian society as well organised as we can conceive possible in this world, the limit would be that our temporal and spiritual life should be harmonised: the temporal and spiritual would never be identified. There would always remain a dual allegiance, to the State and to the Church, to one's countrymen and to one's fellow-Christians everywhere, and the latter would always have the primacy. There would always be a tension: and this tension is essential to the idea of a Christian society, and is a distinguishing mark between a Christian and a pagan society.

The Church of a Christian society, then, should . . . at times . . . be in conflict with the State, in rebuking derelictions in policy, or in defending itself against encroachments of the temporal power, or in shielding the community against tyranny and asserting its neglected rights, or in contesting heretical opinion or immoral legislation and administration. . . .

The obvious secularist solution for muddle is to subordinate everything to political power: and in so far as this involves the subordination of the money-making interests to those of the nation as a whole, it offers some immediate, though perhaps illusory relief. . . . It is only in a society with a religious basis . . . that you can get the proper harmony and tension, for the individual or for the community.

CHAPTER 6

PATRIOTISM AND INTERNATIONALISM

Conservatives believe that the nation-state is the highest form of human organisation that mankind has as yet evolved, and that it is likely to remain so throughout any foreseeable future. They believe that it is not only the interest, but the duty, of every such entity to maintain and defend its own interests. They believe that it is not unreasonable to hope and strive that world politics should be directed by discussion between such entities. They believe that war is always wrong, but that there are things more wrong than war, and that it is, within sanction of conscience, the citizen's duty to bear arms in defence of his country's interests.

In the Conservative tradition, internationalism is regarded not as the converse, but as the child, of nationality. As love of family is the nursery of the love of country, so love of country is the point of departure for the growth of international amity.

(i) *The Little Platoon*

The following passage was cited in Chapter 3, section vi, above; but it is equally relevant here. It comes from Burke's *Reflections on the Revolution*.

The love to the whole is not extinguished by [a] subordinate partiality. Perhaps it is a sort of elemental training to those higher and more large regards, by which alone men come to be affected . . . in the prosperity of a kingdom. . . . To be attached to the subdivision, to love the little platoon we belong to in society, is the first principle . . . of public affections. It is the first link in the series by which we proceed towards a love of our country, and of mankind.

(ii) *Patriotism the basis of Internationalism*

The first sentence below is taken from Coleridge's " Table Talk ", August 14, 1833: the remainder of the paragraph is from *The Friend*, Section I (Political Knowledge), Essay 13; the remainder *ibid.*, Essay 14, and a quotation in J. H. Muirhead's book, *Coleridge as a Philosopher*, pp. 179–180.

The cosmopolitanism which does not spring out of, and blossom upon, the deep-rooted stem of nationality, is a spurious and rotten growth. The patriot knows that patriotism itself is a necessary link in the golden chain of our affections and virtues, and turns away with indignant scorn from the false philosophy or mistaken religion which would persuade him that cosmopolitanism is nobler than nationality, and the human race a sublimer object of love than a people; that Plato, Luther, Newton, and their equals, formed themselves neither in the market nor the senate, but in the world, and for all men of all ages. True! But where, and among whom, are these giant exceptions produced? In the wide empires of Asia, where millions of human beings acknowledge no other bond but that of a common slavery, and are distinguished on the map but by a name which themselves perhaps never heard, or hearing abhor? No! In a circle defined by human affections, the first firm sod within which becomes sacred beneath the quickened step of the returning citizen. . . . Here, and here only, may we confidently expect those mighty minds to be reared and ripened, whose names are naturalised in foreign lands, the sure fellow-travellers of civilisation! and yet render their own country dearer and more proudly dear to their own countrymen. This is indeed cosmopolitanism, at once the nurse and nursling of patriotic affection! . . .

If then in order to be men we must be patriots, and

patriotism cannot exist without national independence, we need no new or particular code of morals to justify us in placing and preserving our country in that relative situation which is most favourable to its independence. . . . It is therefore grounded in the nature of the thing, and not by a mere fiction of the mind, that wise men who have written on the law of nations have always considered the several states of the civilised world as so many individuals, and equally with the latter under a moral obligation to exercise their free agency within such bounds as render it compatible with the existence of free agency in others. . . . Till states are in that self-standingness which admits of reciprocal action, the epoch of international morality is not yet come. . . .

(iii) *Honour, the Handmaid of Humanity*

Wordsworth's tract, "Concerning the Convention of Cintra" (1809), has already been quoted in illustration of Conservative thought on the doctrine of nationality (see Chapter 2, section vii, above). The following passage from the same source affords a fine example of the argument from patriotism to humanity.

For national independence and liberty, and that honour by which these and other blessings are to be preserved, honour—which is no other than the most elevated and pure conception of justice which can be formed, these are more precious than life: else why have we already lost so many brave men in this struggle? . . . If, therefore, by the faculty of reason we can prophesy concerning the shapes which the future may put on,—if we are under the bond of any duty to succeeding generations, there is high cause to guard against a specious sensibility which may encourage a hoarding up of life for its own sake, seducing us from those considerations by which we might learn when it ought to be resigned. Moreover, disregarding future ages, and confining ourselves to the present state of mankind, it may be safely affirmed that he who is the most watchful of the honour of his country, most determined to preserve her fair name at all hazards, will be found, in any view of things which looks beyond the passing hour, the best steward of the *lives* of his countrymen. For, by proving that she is of a firm temper, that she will only submit or yield to a point of her own fixing, and that all beyond is immutable resolution, he will save her from being wantonly attacked; and if attacked, will awe the aggressor into a speedier abandonment of an unjust and hopeless attempt. Thus will he preserve not only that which gives life its value, but life itself ; and not for his own country merely, but for that of his enemies, to whom he will have offered an example of magnanimity which will ensure to them like benefits; an example, the reaction of which will be felt by his own countrymen, and will prevent them from becoming assailants unjustly or rashly. Nations will thus be taught to respect each other, and mutually to abstain from injuries. And hence, by a benign ordinance of our nature, genuine honour is the handmaid of humanity.

(iv) *The Reconciliation of Loyalties*

Arthur Balfour, scholar, philosopher, statesman, was an excellent example of that combination of loyalty to province and country with broad intellectual and humanitarian sympathies which the Conservative tradition, as formulated by Burke and the Romantic Patriots of the early nineteenth century, envisaged as the ideal. A Scottish patriot who passed into law the Education Act of 1902, a maker of the modern conception of the British Commonwealth of Nations, and a promoter of the Zionist movement to re-establish the Jews in Palestine, Lord Balfour was a living example of the mutual interplay of loyalties which he upholds in the following passage from a lecture on "Nationality and Home Rule" in 1913 (*Opinions and Arguments*, London, 1927).

The sentiment of nationality is one of a group of such sentiments for which there is unfortunately no common name. Loyalties to a county, a party, a constitution, a national sovereign, a tribal chief, a church, a race, a creed, are characteristic specimens of the class. They may be ill-directed: they often are. Nevertheless, it is such loyalties that make human society possible; they do more, they make it noble. To them we owe it that a man will sacrifice ease, profit, life itself, for something which wholly transcends his merely personal interests. Therefore, whether mistaken or not, there is always in them a touch of greatness. . . . But it has to be observed that the kind of loyalty we call patriotism, though it expresses a simple feeling, need have no exclusive application. It may embrace a great deal more than a man's country or a man's race. It may embrace a great deal less. And these various patriotisms need not be, and should not be, mutually exclusive. As civilisation advances it becomes more and more necessary for men to learn how loyalties are to be combined without being weakened; how a narrow provincialism is to be avoided on the one hand, and a selfish indifference, masquerading under the name of an enlightened cosmopolitanism, is to be shunned on the other.

As a matter of fact some combination of different patriotisms is almost universal among thinking persons. If I consider the case I know best (namely my own), I find that, within a general regard for mankind, which I hope is not absent or weak, I am moved by a feeling, especially patriotic in its character, for the group of nations who are the authors and the guardians of western civilisation, for the sub-group which speaks the English language, and whose laws and institutions are rooted in British history, for the communities which compose the British Empire, for the United Kingdom of which I am a citizen, and for Scotland where I was born, and is my home, as it was the home of my father before me. If patriotisms such as these are not forced into antagonism, they may not only be consistent with each other, but they may mutually re-inforce each other; and statesmanship can have no higher aim than to make harmony between them easy and conflict impossible.

(v) *The Nation and International Ideals*

This, and the following two sections, are taken from Kenneth Pickthorn's *Principles and Prejudices* (1943). Taken in conjunction with the passages from Coleridge and Wordsworth, above, they show the constancy of the Conservative tradition over the last hundred-and-fifty years. The first bears witness to Conservative realism with regard to international ideals and to Conservative belief in the national entity as the basis of peaceful life among states.

[It will be asked:] are there not much higher things to be fought for than the British Empire? to make the world safe for democracy, for instance, or to make the rule of law universal? must we not grant a League of Nations a higher claim on our allegiance than to our own country? and are not Conservatives visibly self-condemned if they take lower ground than other parties?

The ground is not lower: that absence of compulsion by force which in domestic politics is the prime essence of liberty, in international affairs is called peace. It is tempting to believe that it can be got in the same way as domestic liberty, by centralising and strengthening government; and so, perhaps, it can, but certainly not for a long time yet, until there has been a change of heart, or rather of many million hearts. . . . When the world is as much unified as England was in the sixteenth century, some super-Tudor may centralise world authority as successfully as Henry VIII and Elizabeth centralised English authority, and with as little and as pardonable violence and fraud. When desire for order, when public and private loyalty, when confidence in authority, are as habitual the world over as they were in England a hundred years ago, then armed force may be centralised and universalised and at the same time domesticated. . . .

Meanwhile, it is not unreasonable to believe that political authority, government whose last resource is force, can be most widely exercised and most lightly borne where its basis is national and traditional. It is not unreasonable to believe that the British Government is as large and as good an example of this truth as any. And it is not unreasonable to believe that where a wider area than the British Empire or the Russian Empire is concerned, there authority should be sought in negotiation between governments and not in any super-state or in any written rules that are to have the force of a fixed world-constitution. In short, there is no baseness in supposing that the true internationalism consists in this: to make your own nation as nearly as possible an entity governed by consent and asking from other nations nothing but neighbourliness, and to ensure that so far as in you lies there shall be no reason why world politics should not be directed by discussion between such entities.

(vi) *Britain's Interests are Britain's Business*
This passage contains the principles on which so-called "Conservative" foreign policy have rested at all times.

[Our] highest duty (apart from the direct relation of each one's soul to God) is to defend this country, this empire of which the essence is communication, and to defend also every promise made in the name of this country or empire in pursuance of that defence. . . . Our clearest duty is the choosing of governors who will not say more than they mean nor promise more than they reasonably think our States can perform. The last thing we should tolerate from them would be that they should make any use of the power they owe to us for the purpose of imposing on foreigners their notions of morality, or even of the proper relations between foreigners: no Conservative statesman is likely to say, " We have to exercise British moral leadership for the regeneration of the world, and, when we have got Europe tidied up, then America will come in." No British statesman should feel himself authorised to spend British blood for the promotion of something superior to British interests. If a man doubts that British interests can be defended without prejudice to the highest concerns, British government is not his affair.

Not merely is it not immoral for the foreign policy of the British Government to be concerned with British interests, but it would be immoral and impertinent and foolish (and to all foreigners incredible) that it should be concerned with anything else. Only, it should be directed by honest men honestly concerned with honest interests. . . .

[No Conservative will] be persuaded that what are called ideas or ideals, even when they are more than mere vague modish notions, are better worth fighting for than his country. Luther was not always wrong, certainly not when he said that all wars were legitimate except Holy Wars: the worst thing a man can use force for is to enforce his own notions, and a government could not use force worse than by way of forcing its subjects to force its notions upon foreigners. Such an attempt is not legitimised because the government in question is convinced that the majority of its subjects agree with it, and such an attempt is not only illegitimate but manifestly absurd when the notions to be enforced are dignified with the name of liberty. A man should not quite always fight for his country; he should fight for nothing less, and higher things are not to be fought for.

(vii) *The Nation's Cause and the Citizen's Conscience*
This passage may stand as the classic statement of Conservative thought on conscientious objection in time of war.

When a country is at war, what is the duty of the subjects? . . . The Conservative might do worse than say " my country, right or wrong," and, indeed, a long way in that direction he is bound to go by his prejudice for his country because it *is* his country, and by his prejudice against current assumptions because they are current; he has also other reasons for going the same way. . . .

The Conservative does not doubt the value of the political society, supreme among material values and respectable above material values; he especially respects the value of that traditional society which is the nation and which has the strongest title in time and the widest validity in space; the Conservative, not doubting but not uncritical, and not inactive in forming the mind of the national society, will, when His Majesty's

Government is at war, be inclined to believe that His Majesty's Government is right, or at any rate right enough, that is, more right than its enemy; if he finds this difficult to believe, he will be inclined to think himself more likely to be mistaken than his country's authorised representatives and governors; if he finds his country's rightness impossible to believe, still he will not necessarily believe that duty compels him to withhold co-operation. . . .

The Conservative, incapable of forgetting that human individuality is government's highest concern, cannot be unaware that his own individual judgment is inconceivable out of the context of his country, and that, if he is capable at all of forming an opinion, this capacity cannot be isolated from the promptings of ancestral voices and the resources of communal thought and sentiment. . . .

You may not fight for your country when you are quite sure that that would mean fighting against your religion, but even then you may not fight against your country. . . . The misfortune is conceivable which confronts a man's country with his conscience, so that his soul forbids him to fight for his king and his kin or to execute actively other lawful orders of government; the Conservative will not therefore conclude that such misfortune authorises disobedience. His obedience will continue even if it can be no more than passive, that is to say, acquiescent not in the rightness of commands which his conscience forbids him to execute but in the rightness of his own submission to the consequences of non-co-operation. He will recognise that since his only excuse for withholding full obedience is that he is restrained by motives above material calculation, therefore he cannot complain of material consequences however grievous: material consequences are irrelevant to the considerations to which he has appealed.

A man will be something of a prig or something of a crook or really too much of a fool (or most commonly all three at once), if he very readily argues that higher authority forbids him to obey the commands of his country's legitimate government, orders him to resist that society of which he is an organic member, of which he is a little creator and very largely the creature. To such argument an honest and sensible man *may*, very rarely, be driven. Having been driven so far under such tragic compulsion, he will be persuaded by his sense and his honesty alike that his appeal to eternal values cuts him off from paying or claiming attention to temporal penalties or damages. A man who has it in command from God to light for all humanity a candle that shall never be put out cannot pay to so trivial a matter as his own incineration so much attention as would be involved in complaining about it.

Part II

THE TRADITION
AND THE CHANGING WORLD

When it is not necessary to change, it is necessary not to change.
                                                              FALKLAND

If there is any one eminent criterion, which above all the rest, distinguishes a wise government from an administration weak and im-
provident, it is this: " well to know the best time and manner of
yielding what it is impossible to keep. . . ."
  All the reformations we have hitherto made have proceeded upon
the principle of reference to antiquity; and I hope, nay I am persuaded,
that all those which may possibly be made hereafter, will be carefully
formed upon analogical precedent, authority, and example.
  People will not look forward to posterity, who never look backward
to their ancestors. . . .
  One of the first and most leading principles on which the commonwealth
and the laws are consecrated, is lest the temporary possessors and life-
renters in it, unmindful of what they have received from their ancestor
and of what is due to their posterity, should act as if they were the
entire masters. . . .   EDMUND BURKE

In a progressive country change is constant; and the great question is,
not whether you should resist change which is inevitable, but whether
that change should be carried out in deference to the manners, the
customs, the laws, the traditions of the people, or in deference to abstract
principles and arbitrary and general doctrines.   BENJAMIN DISRAELI

I am a Conservative because I am absolutely certain that no community
in this world has ever flourished, or could ever flourish, if it was faithless
to its own past. What does Conservative mean? It means that the
population of this country feels that it has inherited a great tradition,
and means to use that tradition, not in any spirit of slavish conformity
to ideas which in their particular form might be outworn, but because
they are determined to build solidly for the future, and they know that
unless they build solidly on the past their building will never stand the
stress and storm by which every living community, every great historical
nation, is from time to time threatened.   ARTHUR BALFOUR

The essentially conservative element in Toryism . . . is simply a sense
of the continuity of society, a disbelief in the possibility of a sudden
change or a realisation of its dangers. To call it " conservative " is
really to mistake its character, for it is precisely because a man is not
content with the ground on which he stands and is determined to get
somewhere else that he distrusts short-cuts. . . . Tory radicalism is of
the kind indicated by an Irish-American socialist, reconverted to his
ancestral Church: " I have discovered that, if you believe in God, you
thereby acquire the right to question everything else."
                                          LORD EUSTACE PERCY

A Conservative is a man who believes that in politics the onus of proof
is on the proposer of change. . . . Marks of the Conservative temperament
are devotion to place, country, family, institution, rather than to notions
or fashions, capacity rather for affection and fidelity than for philanthropy
and apprehension, power for adapting means to long-desired ends rather
than for thinking out new purposes.   KENNETH PICKTHORN

127

CHAPTER I

POLITICAL CHANGE:
(I) CONSERVATISM ON
THE DEFENSIVE, 1772–1832

Lord Hugh Cecil has described modern Conservatism as " a force called into activity by the French Revolution, and operating against the tendencies that that Revolution set up ". In these years, therefore, Conservatism—as represented by Burke, Liverpool, Canning, Coleridge and Peel—was chiefly concerned to uphold the historic, prescriptive constitution of " Mixed and balanced powers " against schemes of theoretical perfection based on the doctrine of natural rights and the ideal of simple, or numerical, democracy. This involved the repudiation of the notion of political power as a " mandate from the people "; the insistence that Members of Parliament are not delegates but representatives; and the championship of the independence of the duly elected representatives of the Commons as members of a deliberative assembly, responsible to their own reason and consciences, and not subject to " pressure from without ". Thus Conservatism performed, at the expense of manifold charges of being " reactionary " and obstructive, the negative function of supplying what Peel called " the *vis inertiae* in the machine of government ", and the rather more positive function of criticising new doctrine in the light of tradition. It may have made change slow, but it also made it continuous, thus " preserving ", as Burke put it, " the method of nature in the conduct of the state " so that " in what we improve, we are never wholly new; in what we retain, we are never wholly obsolete."

(i) *Burke on the Position of an M.P.*
From Burke's speech to the Electors of Bristol after the Poll on November 3, 1774.

Certainly, gentlemen, it ought to be the happiness and glory of a representative to live in the strictest union, the closest correspondence, and the most un-reserved communication with his constituents. Their wishes ought to have great weight with him; their opinions high respect; their business unremitted attention. . . . But his unbiassed opinion, his mature judgment, his enlightened conscience, he ought not to sacrifice to you, or to any set of men living. These he does not derive from your pleasure; no, nor from the Law and the constitution. They are a trust from Providence, for the abuse of which he is deeply answerable. Your representative owes you, not his industry alone, but his judgment; and he betrays, instead of serving you, if he sacrifices it to your opinion.

My worthy colleague says his will ought to be sub-servient to yours. If that be all, the thing is innocent. If government were a matter of will upon any side, yours, without question, ought to be superior. But government and legislation are matters of reason and judgment, and not of inclination; and what sort of reason is that, in which the determination precedes the discussion; in which one set of men deliberate and another decide; and where those who form the con-clusion are perhaps three hundred miles distant from those who hear the arguments?

To deliver an opinion is the right of all men; that of constituents is a weighty and respectable opinion, which a representative ought always to rejoice to hear; and which he ought always most seriously to consider. But *authoritative* instructions, *mandates* issued, which the member is bound blindly and implicitly to obey, to vote, or to argue for, though contrary to the clearest conviction of his judgment and conscience—these are things utterly unknown to the laws of this land, and which arise from a fundamental mistake of the whole order and tenor of our constitution.

Parliament is not a *congress* of ambassadors from different and hostile interests . . . but parliament is a *deliberative* assembly of *one* nation, with *one* interest, that of the whole; where not local purposes, not local prejudices, ought to guide, but the general good, resulting from the general reason of the whole. You choose a member indeed; but when you have chosen him, he is not member of Bristol, but he is a member of *parliament*.

(ii) *Burke on the Fallibility of Numbers*

When Burke said farewell to his Bristol constituents in 1780 after differing with them on matters like the Irish Trade and Catholic Relief, he told them: " I am to look indeed to your opinions, but to such opinions as you and I must have five years hence." He proceeded to deny with prophetic vigour the heresy " that the opinions of even the greatest multitudes are the standard of rectitude. . . ."

As to the opinion of the people, which some think, in such cases, is to be implicitly obeyed . . . when we know that the opinions of even the greatest multitudes are the standard of rectitude, I shall think myself obliged to make those opinions the masters of my conscience. But if it may be doubted whether Omnipotence itself is competent to alter the essential constitution of right and wrong, sure I am that such *things*, as they and I, are possessed of no such power. No man carries further than I do the policy of making government pleasing to the people. . . . But I will never act the tyrant for their amusement.

(iii) *Burke on Expert Government*

Perhaps the clearest statement of Burke's views on the expert nature of government occurs in his speech on Economical Reform, February 11, 1780.

The people are the masters. They have only to express their wants at large and in gross. We are the expert artists: we are the skilful workmen, to shape their desires into perfect form, and to fit the utensil to the use. They are the sufferers, they tell the symptoms of the complaint; but we know the exact seat of the disease, and how to apply the remedy according to the rules of art. . . .

In my opinion, it is our duty, when we have the desires of the people before us, to pursue them, not in the spirit of literal obedience, which may militate with their very principle, much less to treat them with a peevish and contentious litigation, as if we were averse parties in a suit. It would, sir, be most dishonourable for a faithful representative of the Commons to take advantage of any inartificial expression of the people's wishes, in order to frustrate their attainment of what they have an undoubted right to expect. We are under infinite obligations to our constituents, who have raised us to so distinguished a trust and have imparted such a degree of sanctity to common characters, we ought to walk before them with purity, plainness and integrity of heart; with filial love, and not with slavish fear, which is always a low and tricking thing. For my own part, in what I have meditated upon that subject, I cannot indeed take it upon me to say I have the honour *to follow* the sense of the people. The truth is, *I met it on the way,* while I was pursuing their interest according to my own ideas.

(iv) *Peel on " Pressure from Without "*

From Sir Robert Peel's speech on the third reading of the Great Reform Bill, September 21, 1831.

To repeat to us, night after night, that the people demand this change, and that, whether for good or evil, it must be made, is anything but satisfactory to a rational and dispassionate mind. We are here to consult the interests, and not to obey the will of the people, if we honestly believe that that will conflict with those interests. It is to invert the relation of the people to their representatives if we are to exclude all exercise of our unfettered judgment, all calculation of probable consequences, and to yield without resistance and against our reason to the prevailing, perhaps the temporary, current of popular feelings. . . . Where is the madman who would refuse compliance with these demands of the people on any ground of private interest—of the loss of borough influence by this peer, or that great proprietor—on any ground, in short, but the honest one of rational doubt whether the change required is for the general and permanent good? If that doubt be sincerely entertained, it cannot be satisfactorily resolved by the vain repetition " the people will have this bill, and you must pass it ".

(v) *Burke defends the unreformed House of Commons as " a legislative body corporate by prescription " against the advocates of " a representation on the principle of numbers "*

From Burke's speech on a motion for a Committee to enquire into the state of representation of the Commons in Parliament, May 7, 1782. It should be noted that Burke was speaking seven years before the outbreak of the French Revolution, which is sometimes said to account for this type of defence of the unreformed House of Commons.

Our constitution is a prescriptive constitution whose sole authority is that it has existed time out of mind. . . . The House of Commons is a legislative body-corporate by prescription, not made upon any given theory, but existing prescriptively—just like the rest. This prescription has made it essentially what it is, an aggregate collection of three parts, knights, citizens, burgesses. . . . A prescriptive government such as ours never was the work of any legislator, never was made upon any foregone theory. . . . I have no more doubt than I entertain of my existence that this . . . is the means of the preservation of our constitution while it lasts; of curing it of many of the disorders which, attending every species of institution, would attend the principle of an exact local representation, or a representation on the principle of numbers. . . . But it is not an arithmetical inequality with which we ought to trouble ourselves. . . . Now, I ask, what advantage do you find that the places which abound in representation possess over others in which it is more scanty, in security for freedom, in security for justice, or in any one of those means of procuring temporal prosperity and eternal happiness, the ends for which society was formed? . . . You have an equal representation, because you have men equally interested in the prosperity of the whole, who are involved in the general interest and the general sympathy. . . .

On the other side there are two parties. . . . The one is juridical, the other political. The one is in the nature of a claim of right, on the supposed rights of man as man. . . . The other ground, as far as I can divine what it directly means, is, that the representation is not so politically framed as to answer the theory of its institution. . . . The first claims a personal representation, the latter rejects it with scorn and fervour. The language of the first party is plain and intelligible; they who plead an absolute right cannot be satisfied with anything short of personal representation, because all *natural* rights must be the rights of individuals; as by nature there is no such thing as politic or corporate personality! all these ideas are mere fictions of law, they are creatures of voluntary institution; men as men are individuals, and nothing else. They, therefore, who reject the principle of natural and personal representation are essentially and eternally at variance with those who claim it. As to the first sort of reformers, it is ridiculous to talk to them of the British constitution upon any or upon all of its bases; for they lay it down that every man ought to govern himself, and that where he cannot go himself he must send his representative; that all other government is usurpation, and is so far from having a claim to our obedience, it is not only our right but our duty to resist it. Nine-tenths of the reformers argue thus, that is, on the natural right. If this claim be founded, it is clear to what it goes. The House of Commons, in that light, undoubtedly is no representative of the people as a collection of individuals. Nobody pretends it is, nobody can justify such an assertion. When you come to examine into this claim of right, founded on the right of self-government in each individual, you find the thing demanded infinitely short of the principle of the demand. . . .

The great object of most of these reformers is to prepare the destruction of the constitution by disgracing and discrediting the House of Commons. For they think, prudently, in my opinion, that if they can persuade the nation that the House of Commons is so constituted as not to secure the public liberty; not to have a proper connexion with the public interests; so constituted as not either actually or virtually to be representative of the people, it will be easy to prove that a government composed of a monarchy, an oligarchy chosen by the crown, and such a House of Commons, whatever good can be in such a system, can by no means be a system of free government.

(vi) *William Pitt, the Younger, on Representation*

Burke's speech, from which the previous passage was taken, was delivered on a motion introduced by the younger Pitt. Pitt was, at this time (1782–83), an advocate of a moderate reform of representation. It was the French Revolution that associated him with the politics and policies which we now know as those of the Tory Party. He followed up his lost motion of 1782 by submitting Resolutions for a moderate measure of reform in the following year. In his speech, May 7, 1783, however, he expressly disavowed universal suffrage, and gave his support to very much the same view of the nature of the House of Commons as a representative body corporate by prescription as was expressed by Burke in the passages quoted in section v, above.

Among the various expedients that have been devised to bar the entrance of such influence, i.e. of the Crown, into that House . . . one is, to extend the right of voting for members to serve in Parliament, which is now so confined, to all the inhabitants of the kingdom indiscriminately, so that every man, without the distinction of freeholder, or freeman of a corporation, shall have the franchise of a vote for a person to represent him in Parliament—and this mode, I understand, is thought by those who patronize it to be the only one that is consistent with true liberty in a free constitution, where everyone ought to be governed by those laws only to which all have actually given their consent, either in person, or by their representative. For myself, I utterly reject and condemn this mode, which it is impossible for me to adopt without libelling those renowned forefathers who had framed the constitution in the fullness of their wisdom and fashioned it for the government of freemen, not of slaves. If this doctrine shall obtain, nearly one half of the people must in fact be slaves; for it is absolutely impossible that this idea of giving to every man a right of voting, however finely it may appear in theory, can ever be reduced to practice. But, though it were even practicable, still one half of the nation would be slaves; for all those who vote for the unsuccessful candidates cannot, in the strictness of this doctrine, be said to be represented in Parliament; and therefore they are governed by laws to which they give not their assent, either in person, or by representatives; consequently, according to the ideas of the friends to this expedient, all those who vote for unsuccessful candidates must be slaves; nay, it is oftentimes still harder with those who are members of Parliament, who are made slaves also, and are governed by laws to which they not only have not given their consent, but against which they have actually voted.

For my part, my idea of representation is this, that the members once chosen, and returned to Parliament, are, in effect, the representatives of the people at large, as well of those who do not vote at all, or who, having voted, give their votes against them, as of those by whose suffrages they are actually seated in the House. This being therefore my principle I cannot consent to an innovation founded on doctrines subversive of liberty, which in reality go so far as to say, that this House of Commons is not, and that no House of Commons ever has been, a true and constitutional representation of the people; for no House of Commons has yet been elected by all the men in the kingdom. The country has long prospered, and has even attained the summit of glory, though this doctrine has never been embraced; and I hope that no one will ever attempt to introduce it into the laws of England, or treat it in any other light than as a mere speculative proposition, that may be good in theory, but which it would be absurd and chimerical to endeavour to reduce to practice.

(vii) *George Canning in defence of the unreformed House*

On April 25, 1822, Lord John Russell moved in the House of Commons " that the present state of the representation of the people in Parliament requires the most serious consideration of the House." George Canning spoke in opposition to the motion at the call of the House, several other Members who had risen giving way to him. What he said is important as coming from a " Liberal Tory ". His insistence upon the independence of the House as a deliberate body, his rejection of the notion of the House as " the exclusive organ of the people's will ", his distrust of reform according to a theory of perfection, his emphasis on the self-adjustment of the House to the interests of society: these points, suspect by Liberals and Radicals when voiced by Burke, or even Coleridge, acquire a novel prestige and respectability when expressed by the progenitor of Liberal Toryism. Canning's final point, about the capacity of the House of Commons for accommodating itself " silently " though " practically " to the prevailing interests of society, is taken up by Coleridge in the next section (viii).

If I contend in behalf of the constitution of the House of Commons such as it is, I contend at least for no untried, no discredited, no confessedly pernicious establishment. I contend for a House of Commons, the spirit of which, whatever be its frame, has, without forcible alteration, gradually, but faithfully, accommodated itself to the progressive spirit of the country. . . . For my part, Sir, I value the system of

Parliamentary Representation for that very want of uniformity which is complained of . . . ; for the variety of rights of election. I conceive that to establish one uniform right would inevitably be to exclude some important interests from the advantage of being represented in this House.

The noble lord has himself stated that in the instance of the Revolution, the Parliament did wisely in setting at naught the immediate feelings of its constituents. There cannot indeed be the slightest doubt that had the nation been polled in 1688, the majority would have been found adverse to the change that was then effected in the Government; but Parliament, acting in its higher and larger capacity, decided for the people's interests against their prejudices. It is not true, therefore, that the House of Commons is necessarily defective because it may not instantly respond to every impression of the people. . . . And it would, in my opinion, be a base and cowardly House of Commons, unworthy of the large and liberal confidence without which it must be incompetent to the discharge of its high functions, which having, after due deliberation, adopted a great public measure, should be frightened back into an acquiescence with the temporary excitement which might exist upon that measure out of doors. . . . If the House has . . . increased in power, is it therefore necessary that it should become more popular in its formation? I should say just the reverse. If it were to add to its real, active, governing influence such an exclusively popular character and tone of action as would arise from the consciousness that it was the immediately deputed agent for the whole people, and the exclusive organ of their will, the House of Commons, instead of enjoying one third part of the power of the state, would in a little time absorb the whole. How could the House of Lords, a mere assembly of individuals, however privileged, and representing only themselves, presume to counteract the decisions of the delegates of the people? How could the Crown itself holding its power, as I should say, *for* the people, but deriving it altogether, as others would contend, *from* the people, presume to counteract, or hesitate implicitly to obey, the supreme authority of the nation assembled within these walls? . . .

If this House is adequate to the functions which really belong to it—which functions are, not to exercise an undivided, supreme dominion in the name of the people, over the Crown and the other branch of the legislature, but checking the one and balancing the other, to watch over the people's rights and to provide especially for the people's interests . . . the mode of its composition appears to me a consideration of secondary importance. . . .

Man himself is said by inspired authority to be " fearfully " as well as " wonderfully made ". The study of anatomy, while it leads to the most beneficial discoveries for the detection and cure of physical disease, has yet a tendency, in some minds, rather to degrade than to exalt the opinion of human nature. . . . So, in considering too curiously the composition of this House and the different processes through which it is composed . . . a dissector of political constitutions might well be surprised to behold the product of such elements in an assembly, of which, whatever may be its other characteristics, no man will seriously deny that it comprehends as much of intellectual ability and of moral integrity as was ever brought together in the civilised world. . . .

By reforming "on principle" I mean, reforming with a view not simply to the redress of any partial, practical grievance, but generally to theoretical improvement. I may add that even "on principle" his [i.e. the noble Lord's] endeavours to reform will be utterly vain if he insists upon the exclusion of influence as an indispensable quality of his reformed constitution. Not in this country only, but in every country in which a popular elective assembly has formed part of the Government, to exclude such influences from the elections has been a task either not attempted or attempted to no purpose. While we dam up one source of influence, a dozen others will open; in proportion as the progress of civilisation, the extension of commerce, and a hundred other circumstances, better understood than defined, contribute to shift and change, in their relative proportions, the prevailing interests of society. Whether the House of Commons, in its present shape, does not practically though silently accommodate itself to such changes with a pliancy almost as faithful as the nicest artifice could contrive, is, in my opinion, I confess, a much more important consideration than whether the component parts of the House might be arranged with neater symmetry or distributed in more scientific proportions. . . . A search after abstract perfection in government may produce, in generous minds, an enterprise and enthusiasm to be recorded by the historian and to be celebrated by the poet: but such perfection is not an object of reasonable pursuit because it is not one of possible attainment. . . .

(viii) *Coleridge on the self-adjustment of Representation*

A critic of the Constitution in a profoundly philosophical sense, Coleridge was yet a Conservative in his awareness of the organic continuity of institutions. He pointed out that within a living and organic constitution certain more or less automatic self-adjustments take place with time. Disturbance of balance tended to correct itself by a necessary process of redistribution of weight. He thought that these "natural" processes should be taken into account by reformers, even if only as signs and symptoms of unhealth, pointing out "the places in the body politic which need a remodelling of the law". This was, perhaps, a more subtle exposition of what Canning and Peel referred to when they spoke of the need for caution in tampering with so mighty and complex a piece of mechanism as a constitution, and the existence of "detached movements which we do not comprehend . . ." (see vii, above, and ix, following).

The following passages are taken: (a) from Chapter II of *The Constitution of the Church and State according to the Idea of Each*; (b) from "Table Talk", September 19, 1830, June 25, 1831, and May 21, 1832.

(a)

That the burgesses were not bound to elect representatives from among their own order . . . that the elective-franchise of the towns, ports, etc., first invested with borough-rights, was not made conditional . . . on their retaining the same comparative wealth and independence . . . that in consequence of these and other causes, the very weights intended for the effectual counterpoise of the great landholders have in the course of events been shifted into the opposite scale . . . these are no part of the constitution, no essential ingredients in the idea, but apparent defects and imperfections in its realisation—which, however, we will neither regret nor set about amending, till we have seen whether an equivalent force had not arisen to supply the deficiency. . . . Roads, canals, machinery, the press, the periodical and daily press, the might of public opinion, the consequent increasing desire of popularity among public men and functionaries of every description, and the increasing necessity of public character as a means or condition of political influence —I need but mention these to stand acquitted of having started a vague and naked possibility in extenuation of an evident and palpable abuse. . . .

(b)

It has never yet been seen, or clearly announced, that democracy, as such, is no proper element in the constitution of a state. . . . Democracy is the healthful life-blood which circulates through the veins and arteries, which supports the system, but which ought never to appear externally, as the mere blood itself. . . . In that imperfect state of society in which our system of representation began, the interests of the country were pretty exactly commensurate with its municipal divisions. . . . The democracy of England . . . was where it ought to be, in the corporations, the vestries, the joint-stock companies. . . . The counties, the towns, and the sea-ports, accurately enough represented the only interests then existing; that is to say, the landed, the shop-keeping or manufacturing, and the mercantile. But for a century past, at least, this division has become notoriously imperfect, some of the most vital interests of the empire being now totally unconnected with any English localities. Yet now, when the evil and the want are known, we are to abandon the accommodations which the necessity of the case had worked out for itself, and begin again with a rigidly territorial plan of representation! . . . Undoubtedly it is a great evil that there should be such an evident discrepancy between the law and the practice of the constitution in the matter of the representation. Such a direct, yet clandestine[1], contravention of solemn resolutions and established laws is immoral, and greatly injurious to the cause of legal loyalty and general subordination in the minds of the people. But then, a statesman should consider that these very contraventions of law in practice point out to him the places in the body politic which need a remodelling of the law. You acknowledge a certain necessity for indirect representation in the present day, and that such representation has been instinctively obtained by means contrary to law; why then do you not approximate the useless law to the useful practice, instead of abandoning both law and practice for a completely new system of your own?

(ix) *Peel sums up*

Speaking on Lord John Russell's Motion to give representatives to Manchester, Birmingham and Leeds, on February 23, 1830, Peel stood firmly by the Conservative tradition of Burke and Canning. The first passage below is taken from this speech. The second is taken from his speech in the Commons on the introduction of the Reform Bill, March 3, 1831, and is included as an illustration of the use, by an " enlightened " Conservative, of the Burkian doctrine of " prescription ", and for Peel's references to " detached movements " within the constitutional machine. Peel's extended criticism of the Reform Bill is given in the next chapter.

Having maturely weighed those powerful arguments which were first brought forward by Mr. Burke, and afterwards, no less ably, by my late right hon. friend Mr. Canning, I confess that they have established, to my mind, conclusive proof of the great danger that there is in tampering, on slight grounds, with the constitution. I think that the arguments of those two great

---

[1] Coleridge appears to be referring to the practice, on the part of unrepresented interests, of " retaining " the services of Members elected for decayed boroughs.

men,—that we are not to seek the principles of the representation of the House of Commons, either in any finespun theories of democracy, or in any of the institutions of the free republics of ancient times, and that we cannot find in any portion of the history of England any principle of democratic representation to serve as a model for a reconstruction of the representative system,—I think, I say, that those arguments are decisive upon the points for which they are advanced. . . .

The noble lord has pointed out the theoretical defects in our present system of representation; he has appealed to the people; he has desired them to accompany him to the green moulds of Old Sarum and the ruined niches of Midhurst. I, too, make my appeal to the same people; I ask them, when they have finished poring over the imputed blots in their form of government, when they have completed their inspection of the impurities of Old Sarum, and Gatton, and Midhurst;—I ask them to elevate their vision, *os homini sublime dedit*, to include within their view a wider range than that to which the noble lord would limit them. I ask them to look back upon a period of one hundred and fifty years—to bear in mind that their constitution in its present form has so long endured; and I ask them where, among the communities of Europe, do you find institutions which have afforded the same means of happiness and the same security for liberty? I conjure them to bear in mind the result of every attempt that has hitherto been made to imitate our own institutions. In France, in Spain, in Portugal, in Belgium, the utmost efforts have been exhausted to establish a form of government like ours—to adjust the nice balance between the conflicting elements of royal, aristocratical, and popular power,—to secure the inestimable blessings of limited monarchy and temperate freedom.

I hope that the people of England will consider that the constitution of a government is a matter of extreme delicacy and importance, not to be judged of by the examination of any isolated part, which may be put forward for the purpose of exciting abhorrence; but demanding a comprehensive view, not only of the structure as a whole, but of its practical effects. It was well said by Mr. Canning . . . that in judging of any form of government, we should bring to the consideration of it the same caution, the same distrust in our own knowledge, with which we should pronounce upon some mighty and complex piece of mechanism. There may be detached movements that we do not comprehend,—movements which, to the superficial and ignorant, may seem not only useless but pernicious; but surely we must not condemn them, if there be harmony in the working of the whole machine, and if its objects be completely effected.

CHAPTER 2

POLITICAL CHANGE:
(II) CONSERVATISM AT THE CRISIS OF 1832—AND AFTER

Once the Great Reform Bill had become law, Conservatism loyally accepted and enforced it, thereby dissociating itself from "Reaction" of the Continental type, which prides itself on its irreconcilability, and thereby condemns itself to a merely negative (and often disloyal) part in the national life. Conservatism adapted itself to the new situation, took its place within it, and brought to bear upon it its own characteristic gifts of adaptation, constructive criticism and historic sense. In so doing, Conservatism emerged as the precise and literal label of a party and a creed. Under Peel's guidance, it went out to win the new electorate, and to identify itself with the national, as distinct from a sectional, interest. Peel's patient work made this possible; Disraeli's imaginative opportunism brought it to fruition. The second Reform Bill, in 1867, was delivered to the nation by a Conservative Party that could justly claim to be the national party. Thereafter, the adaptation of the tradition to political change was complete.

(i) *Coleridge on the desertion of principle*

Coleridge, like Burke, held that the principle of our representative system was the representation not of persons but of interests. While he was prepared for an extension of the suffrage and for a redistribution of seats, he pleaded for a reform of the system according to its inherent principle. To enfranchise the £10 householder was, to him, mere "political empiricism" of the worst kind. The following passages are taken from his "Table Talk", 1830–1832.

Is the House of Commons to be reconstructed on the

146

principle of a representation of interests, or of a delegation of men? If on the former, we may perhaps see our way; if on the latter, you can never, in reason, stop short of universal suffrage; and in that case I am sure that women have as good a right to vote as men. . . . The miserable tendency of all is to destroy our nationality, which consists, in a principal degree, in our representative government, and to convert it into a degrading delegation of the populace. There is no unity for a people but in a representation of national interests; a delegation from the passions or wishes of the individuals themselves is a rope of sand.

This Reform Bill seems the *ne plus ultra* of that tendency of the public mind which substitutes its own undefined notions or passions for real objects and historical actualities. There is not one of the ministers —except the one or two revolutionists among them— who has even given us a hint, throughout this long struggle, as to what he really does believe will be the product of the Bill; what sort of House of Commons it will make for the purpose of governing this Empire soberly and safely. No; they have actualised for a moment a wish, a fear, a passion, but not an idea.

Government is not founded on property, taken merely as such, in the abstract; it is founded on *unequal* property; the inequality is the essential term in the position. The phrases—higher, middle, and lower classes, with reference to this point of representation— are delusive. There is an indissoluble blending and interfusion of persons from top to bottom; and no man can trace a line of separation through them, except such a confessedly unmeaning and unjustifiable line of political empiricism as £10 householders. I cannot discover a ray of principle in the Government plan. . . .

(ii) *The constitutional dangers of the manner of passing the Bill*

Conservative critics like Coleridge and Peel thought that the *manner* in which the Whigs passed the Bill—i.e. by appealing to and giving way to, mass opinion; by threatening the House of Lords with the creation of new Peers to swamp opposition; and by implicating King William IV in their designs—had opened the door to future constitutional changes of a fatally revolutionary nature.

Coleridge expressed himself thus, in his "Table Talk" November 20, 1831, and May 20, 1832.

The Bill is bad enough, God knows; but the arguments of its advocates, and the manner of their advocacy, are a thousand times worse than the Bill itself.... I have heard but two arguments of any weight adduced in favour of passing the Great Reform Bill, and they are in substance these: (1) We will blow your brains out if you don't pass it; (2) We will drag you through a horse-pond if you don't pass it; and there is a good deal of force in both.

The present ministers have, in my judgment, been guilty of two things pre-eminently wicked, *sensu politico*, in their conduct upon this Reform Bill. First, they have endeavoured to carry a fundamental change in the material and mode of action of the Government of the country by so exciting the passions, and playing upon the necessary ignorance of the numerical majority of the nation, that all freedom and utility of discussion, by competent heads, in the proper place should be precluded. In doing this they have used, or sanctioned the use of, arguments which may be applied with equal or even greater force to the carrying of any measure whatever, no matter how atrocious in its character or destructive in its consequences. They have appealed directly to the argument of the greater number of voices, no matter whether the utterers were drunk or sober, competent or not competent; and they have done the utmost in their power to rase out the sacred principle in politics of a representation of interests, and to introduce the mad and barbarising scheme of a delegation of individuals. . . .

Secondly, they have made the *King* the prime mover in all this political wickedness; they have made the *King* tell his people that they were deprived of their rights, and, by direct and necessary implication, that they and their ancestors for a century past had been slaves: they have made the King vilify the memory of his own brother and father.

(iii) *Peel, on the same*

In speeches on both the third reading of the Reform Bill in the House of Commons and on the Commons' Consideration of the Lords' Amendments (September 21, 1831, and June 5, 1832), Peel declared that the arguments which had been used in support of the Bill in the House of Commons might in future be employed against a *reformed* House, and that the threat to create Peers to overcome the resistance of the House of Lords might well be used to destroy the independence of that House itself (which is, more or less, what happened in 1911).

If no practical grievance calls for the change—if we are to make it merely that we may gratify the wishes of the people, or may conform to some more plausible theory of government,—in that case I foresee no stability in the conduct of public affairs—nothing but a series of future changes. The same practical evils will continue to be endured. The people, disappointed in their expectations of relief, will call for new experiments; and what is to be opposed to the demand? What argument used against the present state of representation, will not be urged with equal force against that which is about to be established? Those who attack the present fortress will soon be the garrison of that by which they replace it. It behoves them, before they leave the entrenchment from which their successful assault has been made, to spike their guns, and carefully remove every instrument of offence which has contributed to their victory; for be assured, that there is not one that will not be directed against themselves —that there is not a missile, from the heaviest to the meanest, from the largest shell to the smallest sparrow-shot which has been discharged in the present conflict against this House of Commons, that will not be discharged against its successor.

You may depend upon it that the passing of this measure, in the manner in which it will pass, will form a fatal precedent, one to which a government may again and again recur, for the purpose of procuring assent to other measures which, in obedience to popular clamour, such a government may bring forward. Whenever the government come to deal with the Corn Laws, or other questions calculated to excite the feelings and inflame the passions of the people, the precedents furnished by the present occasion will be appealed to; and if they should be placed in similar circumstances of difficulty and excitement, the necessity of restoring tranquility will be made a plea for menacing, and, if necessary, for destroying the independence of the House of Lords.

(iv) *The Bill as initiating the decline of "Mixed Government" and the rise of "pure democracy"*

When Conservative critics prophesied this change, they were not thinking of the very moderate extension of the franchise involved in the measure, but of the tendencies inherent in the process which the Bill must inevitably initiate. The following passages are from Peel's speeches in the debates on the Reform Bill, September 21, 1831, March 22, 1832, December 17, 1831, and July 6, 1831.

The noble lord says, the bill makes no change in the constitution of the country,—that it leaves untouched the sovereign authority and the functions of the House of Lords; and he consoles us by telling us, that after the bill has passed, we shall have, as we had before, the King, the Lords, and the Commons. But what avails it to retain the name and the form, if the essence and the substance be lost? . . . And when was it that power was usurped—whether that usurpation was effected through the ambition of single men, of oligarchies, or of popular assemblies,—when was it that names and forms were not retained? And for what purpose? Why, to ensure the success of the encroachment—to avoid too violent a shock to the prejudices and feelings of the governed—to pay a dishonest homage to those instincts of our nature which rally round ancient institutions, involuntary and unreasoning affections. What tyrant in ancient history—what successful soldier in modern times—what democratic body aiming at the monopoly of power, has been foolish enough to neglect the outward observance of these politic decencies? . . . This bill does not violate the forms of the constitution. I admit it;—but I assert, that while it respects those forms, it destroys the balance of opposing, but not hostile, powers; that it is a sudden and violent transfer of an authority which has hitherto been shared by all orders of the state in just proportions, exclusively to one. In short, all its tendencies are to substitute for a mixed form of government, a pure unmitigated democracy.

In my opinion the bill will give an additional influence to the democratic power of the state, as distinguished from the Monarchy and the House of Lords, so great as to make that power supreme, and virtually therefore to convert the mixed government under which we have lived into a simple democracy. . . . Hereafter there will be no *vis inertiae* in the machine of government—none of that power of resistance to the restlessness of a desire of perpetual change, which at present results, not only from the monarchial system of government, but from the feelings, habits, and prejudices which are interwoven with ancient prescriptive institutions. The power of the House of Commons will hereafter be supreme; the other branch of the legislature will exist merely by sufferance, until it is discovered that institutions which have merely the shadow and semblance of authority are useless and expensive pageants, and had better be abolished.

I will continue my opposition to the last, believing as I do, that this is the first step, not directly to revolution, but to a series of changes that will affect the property, and totally change the character of the mixed constitution of this country. . . . I will oppose to the last the undue encroachment of that democratic spirit to which we are advised to yield without resistance. We may make it supreme—we may establish a republic full of energy, splendid in talent—but in my conscience I believe, fatal to our liberty, our security and our peace.

It is triumphantly asked, will you not trust the people of England? Do you charge them with disaffection to the monarchy and to the constitution under which they live? I answer, that without imputing disaffection to the people or a deliberate intention on their part to undermine the monarchy, or destroy the peerage, my belief is, that neither the monarchy nor the peerage can resist with effect the decrees of a House of Commons that is immediately obedient to every popular impulse, and that professes to speak the popular will; and that all the tendencies of such an assembly are towards the increase of its own power, and the intolerance of any extrinsic control.

(v) *Wellington prophesies " a fierce democracy "*
    The following passages from a speech by the Duke of Wellington on the second reading of the Reform Bill in the House of Lords, October 4, 1831, afford a counterpart to Peel's speeches in the Commons.

Taking the whole view of this system of representation to be established in England, Scotland, and Ireland, I cannot but consider that the House of Commons returned by it will be a democratical assembly of the worst description; that Radical Reform, Vote by Ballot, and all the evil consequences to be expected from the deliberations of such an assembly, must follow from its establishment. I entreat your Lordships to pause before you agree to establish such a system in your country.

But we are told that the people wish for this measure; and when we express our sense of the danger which attends it on account of the democratical power which it tends to establish, an endeavour is made to calm our apprehensions by the assurance that the people are attached to the Government of King, Lords, and Commons. . . .

But, before we go further, it is desirable that we should examine what is the government of King, Lords, and Commons, as established in this Kingdom. In this Government, the King is at the head of everything. All the power is in his hands. . . . His Ministers are responsible not only for the legality, but for the prudence and fitness of his acts. To whom are they responsible? To this, and the Other House of Parliament, to the latter principally, on account of the greater activity of its inquisitorial power—on account of its possessing exclusively the power of the purse, and for other reasons. Every act of the Government, or of the King, is liable to be brought under discussion in, and is, in fact, controlled by the House of Commons; and, for this reason alone, it is important we should consider of what description of men the House of Commons is likely to be composed, when we are discussing the question of Parliamentary reform, in order that we may be quite certain that they will exercise their high functions with wisdom and discretion. . . . It is only by the influence of property over the elections of members of the House of Commons, and by the influence of the Crown and of this House, and of the property of the country upon its proceedings that the great powers of such a body as the House of Commons can be exercised with discretion and safety. The King could not perform the duties of his high station, nor the House of Lords, if the House of Commons were formed on the principle and plan proposed by this Bill. . . .

A noble Earl [the Earl of Winchilsea] who has spoken on this side of House, has made an observation to your Lordships, which well deserves your attention. The noble Earl has told you that, if you increase but a little the democratic power in the state, the step can never be withdrawn. Your Lordships must continue in the same course till you have passed through the miseries of a revolution, and thence to a military despotism, and the evils which attend that system of government. It is not denied that this Bill must increase beyond measure the democratic power of the state—that it must constitute in the House of Commons a fierce democracy; what must be the consequences your Lordships will judge.

I will not detain your Lordships by adverting to the merits of the system of government which has existed up to the present moment, upon which my opinion is by no means altered. No man denies that we have enjoyed great advantages. . . . If this democratic assembly should once be established in England, does any man believe that we should continue to enjoy these vast advantages? But a democracy has never been established in any part of the world that has not immediately declared war against property—against the payment of the public debt—and against all the principles of conservation, which are secured by and are, in fact, the principal objects of the British Constitution, as it now exists. Property, and its possessors, will become the common enemy. I do not urge this argument as one in which your Lordships are peculiarly interested; it is not you alone, nor even other proprietors, who are interested in the protection of property; the whole people, middling classes as well as the lower orders, are interested in this subject. Look at the anxiety prevailing in every part of London, in respect of the great revolution to be made by this Bill. . . .

If I am right in thinking this fierce democracy will be established in the House of Commons, does any man believe that the harmony can continue between the King and his Government and the House of Commons? . . .

(vi) *Evils of enfranchising shop-keepers*
From Coleridge's "Table Talk", March 3 and February 24, 1832.

I am afraid the Conservative party see but one half of the truth. The mere extension of the franchise is not the evil; I should be glad to see it greatly extended —there is no harm in that, *per se*; the mischief is that the franchise is nominally extended, but to such classes, and in such a manner, that a practical disfranchisement of all above, and a discontenting of all below, a favoured class, are the unavoidable results.

I could not help smiling, in reading the report of Lord Grey's speech in the House of Lords, the other night, when he asked Lord Wicklow whether he seriously believed that he, Lord Grey, or any of the ministers, intended to subvert the institutions of the country. Had I been in Lord Wicklow's place, I should have been tempted to answer this question something in the following way; ". . . You have destroyed the freedom of Parliament; you have done your best to shut the door of the House of Commons to the property, the birth, the rank, the wisdom, of the people, and have flung it open to their passions and their follies. You have disfranchised the gentry, and the real patriotism of the nation; you have agitated and exasperated the mob, and thrown the balance of political power into the hands of that class [the shop-keepers] which, in all countries and in all ages, has been, is now, and ever will be, the least patriotic and the least conservative of any. . . ."

(vii) *Peel accepts the Reform Bill as " a final and irrevocable settlement . . ."*

On assuming office in December 1834, Sir Robert Peel issued an " Address to the Electors of Tamworth "—better known as " The Tamworth Manifesto ". Although the manifesto was addressed to his own constituents, Peel had secured for it the approval of his Cabinet, and it constituted an address to the nation at large proclaiming the principles upon which the new Administration intended to conduct public affairs: loyal acceptance of the Reform Bill in both its terms and its spirit, together with continuing loyalty to ancient institutions and a readiness to correct proved abuses and redress real grievances. In effect, it constituted the charter of the new Conservative Party.

With respect to the Reform Bill itself, I will repeat now the declaration which I made when I entered the House of Commons as a member of the reformed Parliament, that I consider the Reform Bill a final and irrevocable settlement of a great constitutional question— a settlement which no friend to the peace and welfare of this country will attempt to disturb, either by direct or by insidious means. Then as to the spirit of the Reform Bill, and the willingness to adopt and enforce it as a rule of government. If by adopting the spirit of the Reform Bill it be meant that we are to live in a perpetual vortex of agitation—that public men can only support themselves in public estimation by adopting every popular impression of the day, by promising the instant redress of anything which anybody may call an abuse, by abandoning altogether that great aid of government, more powerful than either law or reason, the respect for ancient rights, and the deference to prescriptive authority; if this be the spirit of the Reform Bill, I will not undertake to adopt it. But if the spirit of the Reform Bill implies merely a careful

review of institutions, civil and ecclesiastical, under-
taken in a friendly temper, combining with the firm
maintenance of established rights, the correction of
proved abuses, and the redress of real grievances; in
that case, I can, for myself and colleagues, undertake
to act in such a spirit and with such intentions.

(viii) *Conservative Principles*

The following passages from a speech delivered by Peel at the
Merchant Taylors' Dinner, May 11, 1835, throw further light on
his conception of Conservative principles, and on his historic
achievement in the history of the Party—the attachment to the
Party of "men from whom we had been separated in consequence of differences which no longer existed" and "the
middle class of the community . . . those who are mainly the
depositories of the elective franchise." The speech illustrates
most effectively Peel's part in the transition of Conservatism (or
Toryism) from an aristocratic to a middle-class creed—the
transition which Disraeli was to deplore and to modify but not
to undo.

We are charged with having some interest in the
perpetuation of abuses. Why, can there be anyone with
a greater interest than we have that the public burdens
should be as much lightened as they can possibly be,
consistently with the maintenance of the public engagements? . . . We have a direct, a superior interest to
any other in the correction of every abuse, and the
application of every principle of just and wise economy.
At the same time, consistently with these feelings,
consistently with a determination to correct real abuses,
and to promote real economy, we do not disguise that
it is our firm resolution to maintain to the utmost of
our power the limited monarchy of this country—to
respect the rights of every branch of the legislature—

to maintain inviolate the united Church of England and Ireland. . . . Such is our firm resolution. . . . This is the appeal we make to the middle classes of the community—to those who are mainly the depositaries of the elective franchise. We tell them that it is not only our determination to resist any direct attack on our institutions, but that we are resolved that we will not permit the ancient prescriptive government of this country—the mitigated monarchy, consisting of three branches of the legislature— . . . to be changed by plausible and specious propositions of reform into a democratic republic. We will not allow that, if we can prevent it, through plausible and popular pretexts of improvement and reform, there shall gradually take place such an infusion of democracy into the institutions of this country, as shall essentially change their theory and practical character, and shall by slow degrees rob us of the blessings we have so long enjoyed under our limited monarchy, and popular but balanced constitution. Now, gentlemen, that is what I apprehend we mean by, this is the construction we put upon, the term " Conservative principles " ; and such is the ground on which we make an appeal to the country at large, for the maintenance of those principles. We tell all, in whatever class of life they may be, that they ought to feel as deep an interest in the maintenance of those principles, as any of the politicians or men of property who are now within my hearing. The encouragement of industry, the demand for productive labour, depends on the maintenance of those principles. The preservation of order depends on them, the maintenance of that security which has hitherto led men through honest industry to accumulate property in this country, depends upon them. . . .

159

(ix) *Widening the Foundations*

How important Peel considered the organisation of the new electorate to be for the future of the Conservative Party may be judged from his emphasis, in the following passages from his speech at the Tamworth Dinner of July 28, 1841. (The second paragraph is taken from a speech on a similar occasion in 1837.) These passages express his realistic understanding of the vital importance of an organised electorate in the new political situation created by the Reform Bill.

I said before, and I believe it has been proved to be true, that the battle of the constitution must be fought in the registration courts: I say now that the victory which has been achieved must be secured in the registration courts. I do hope the Conservative Party of this country will continue to secure for themselves, by all fair and legitimate means, and by no other whatever, the possession of that power and influence in the state which their wealth, their intelligence, their character, fully entitle them to exercise. I hope they will carefully consider every franchise to which the law entitles them, and secure to themselves the exercise of it. . . . Their good will and their confidence can be the only safe foundation for political opinion; and if they wish to retain the influence they now possess, it must be by the exertion of the same zeal, and industry, and perseverance, which have placed them in their present position. These are the means by which they can enable those in whom they repose confidence to maintain on their ancient foundations the institutions of the country in Church and State. And let them bear in mind that the more secure these foundations are, the more confidence there may be in their stability, the more easy it will be, without exciting alarm or apprehension, to apply those renovations and those repairs which the lapse of time or altered circumstances may have rendered advisable in our ancient institutions.

It may be disagreeable, and, indeed, inconvenient, to attend to the registration of voters which annually takes place throughout the country. All this may be revolting; but you may depend upon it that it is better you should take that trouble than you should allow the Constitution to become the victim of false friends, or that you should be trampled under the hoofs of a ruthless democracy. The advice which has been given by some persons was, " Agitate, agitate, agitate! " The advice which I give you is this—" Register, register, register! "

CHAPTER 3

POLITICAL CHANGE: (III) CONSERVATISM TAKES THE INITIATIVE

Peel's work had been to reconcile Conservatism to the Reform Bill and to widen its foundations in the new electorate of the middle classes. Disraeli was to claim, and to establish, for Conservatism the initiative in adjusting the representative system to changes in the spirit and structure of society. Peel had identified his ideal of Conservatism with the national interest by repealing the Corn Laws at the (supposed) expense of one section of the community. Disraeli was to teach the party to believe in itself as the hereditary trustee of the national interest. Although he held that Peel had played the Whig game for the benefit of the middle classes (the shop-keepers and the "spinning-jenny fellows") at the expense of the aristocracy and the working classes; although he scoffed at "Conservatism" as a Whiggish sham; although he gloried in the older and bolder name of "Tory"—nevertheless, it was the wise, cautious, patriotic work of Peel in the dangerous years of transition that made Disraeli's work possible. "I had to educate our party," Disraeli said, in 1867. But it was owing to Peel that he had any party to educate.

(i) *Disraeli demands that Conservatism take the initiative*

Peel had still two years to live when Disraeli, the rising parliamentarian of forty-four who had rallied the gentlemen of England against his leader's "betrayal" of the landed interest in repealing the Corn Laws, made his first considered parliamentary utterance on the question of political reform. In the speech from which the following excerpts are taken (June 20, 1848, on Joseph Hume's Motion for Parliamentary Reform), he criticised the Bill of 1832 as a step in the selfish Whig policy of aggrandizing the middle classes at the expense of both the aristocracy and the working classes. He carries on the Conservative tradition of Burke and Coleridge in attacking a suffrage based on mere numbers, of the "political empiricism" of such an arbitrary property qualification as "Ten-pound householders", and insists that the franchise should be based on social realities like "interests"—a premonition of his proposal of "fancy franchises" in 1859 and 1867. Finally, he claimed the leadership of reform for "the Gentlemen of England", the natural leaders of the people, the true exponents of national, as distinct from class or sectional, government.

The suffrage is not a right[1]; it is not even a trust—that vague and canting phrase; it is a privilege. The Commons are a privileged order, and the reform of that order was a reconstruction of that order. The Reform Act was most unsatisfactory to me and my friends, but it was fully supported and sanctioned by the people, and should not be disturbed unless they could be sure of arriving at a new reconstruction which would give satisfaction to the people and security to the State. Not that I am an advocate of finality. The most striking mistake in the settlement of 1832 was that it took property as the only qualification for the exercise of political rights. Hume's project was open to the same objection. There was no educational suffrage, no industrial suffrage, no attempt to increase or vary the elements of suffrage, but property alone was its basis. . . .

This is a middle-class movement to aggrandize the power of that class, at the expense not merely of the aristocracy but of the working classes. What was the

[1] If "right" had anything to do with the matter, Disraeli observed, women must be allowed to vote as well as men. Cf. Coleridge's view, Chapter 2, Section i, above.

history of its legislative enterprise? The middle classes emancipated the negroes, but never proposed the Ten Hours Bill for English workmen. In their Reform Bill they destroyed, under the pretence of its corrupt exercise, the old industrial franchise, and they never constructed a new one. Again in their commercial legislation, while the interests of Capital were unblushingly advocated, the displaced labour of the country was offered neither consolation nor compensation, but was told that it must submit to be absorbed in the mass. There was no evidence in any of these reforms of any sympathy with the working classes. . . .

Why are the people of England forced to find leaders among these persons? The proper leaders of the people are the gentlemen of England. If they are not the leaders of the people, I do not see why there should be gentlemen. . . . My honourable friends around me call themselves the country party. Why, that was the name once in England of a party who were the foremost to vindicate popular rights—who were the natural leaders of the people and the champions of everything national and popular: and you must blame yourselves alone if you have allowed the power that has been entrusted to you by the Constitution to slip from your hands, to be exercised for other interests than the general good of your country. . . . If it be true that we are on the eve of troublous times, if it indeed be necessary that changes should take place in this country, let them be effected by those who ought to be the leaders in all political and social changes. Then we shall not find changes carried into effect for the unblushing purpose of securing a middle-class Government, but an English and a national Government, the pride of the people, and in which confidence can be placed.

(ii) *A Mirror of England*

Disraeli's Parliamentary Reform Bill of 1859 failed, but it is very important as an illustration of the continuity of Conservative thought on this matter of representative government. In his speeches, Disraeli stressed throughout the traditional Conservative doctrine, that representation should not be accorded to numbers but to interests. This was the purpose of his "Fancy Franchises". The House of Commons should be a mirror of English society, not a delegation of numbers. Lastly, reform should be, in true Conservative fashion, "accommodative"—and should not claim "finality", after the Whig fashion, for there could be no finality in a living, changing society. "We must accommodate the settlement of 1832 to the England of 1859," he told Lord Stanley. "I never intended to commit the Government or myself to what is called *finality.*"

The first passage given below is taken from Disraeli's speech begging leave to bring in a reform bill, on February 28, 1859, and contains the points just referred to. The second passage is taken from his reply to critics of the measure at the close of the last night's debate (March 31, 1859), and is included as a fair example of Disraeli's maintenance of the traditional conservative attitude towards manhood suffrage, or mere *numerical* democracy.

If we judge of the Act of 1832 by its consequences, in the measures of this House and in the character of its members, it must be admitted that that policy was equal to the emergency it controlled and directed. . . . But, Sir, it must be remembered that the labours of the statesmen who took part in the transactions of 1832 were eminently experimental. In many respects they had to treat their subject empirically, and it is not to be wondered at if in the course of time it was found that some errors were committed in that settlement; and if, as time rolled on, some, if not many deficiencies, were discovered. I beg the House to consider well those effects of time, and what has been the character of the twenty-five years that have elapsed since the Reform of 1832. They form no ordinary period.

In a progressive country, and a progressive age, progress has been not only rapid, but, perhaps, precipitate. There is no instance in the history of Europe of such an increase of population as has taken place in this country during this period. There is no example in the history of Europe or America, of a creation and accumulation of capital so vast as has occurred in this country in those twenty-five years. And I believe the general diffusion of intelligence has kept pace with that increase of population and wealth. . . . It is therefore not surprising that in a measure passed twenty-five years ago, in a spirit necessarily experimental, however distinguished were its authors, and however remarkable their ability, some omissions have been found that ought to be supplied, and some defects that ought to be remedied. . . .

If the measure we recommend be adopted, you will have a great homogeneous constituency, with much variety of character—for variety in the franchise is perfectly consistent with identity in the suffrage; you will have a great homogeneous body, between the different sections of which there will no longer exist feelings of dissatisfaction and distrust. The electors will elect a man of the community in which he lives, and he will exercise the right under the high sense of duty that influences Englishmen in performing it. I have always thought the ideal of the constituent body in England should be this—it should be numerous enough to be independent, and select enough to be responsible. . . .

You want in this House every element that obtains respect and engages the interest of the country. You must have lineage and great territorial property; you must have manufacturing enterprise of the highest character; you must have commercial weight; you must have professional ability in all its forms; but you want something more—you want a body of men not too ultimately connected either with agriculture, or with manufactures, or with commerce; not too much wedded to professional thought and professional habits; you want a body of men representing the vast variety of the English character: men who would arbitrate between the claims of those great predominant interests, who would temper the acerbity of their controversies. You want a body of men to represent that immense portion of the community who cannot be ranked under any of those striking and powerful classes to which I have referred, but who are in aggregate equally important and valuable, and perhaps as numerous . . . a mirror of the mind as well as the material interests of England.

I have no apprehension myself that, if you had manhood suffrage to-morrow, the honest, brave and good-natured people of England would resort to pillage, incendiarism, and massacre. Who expects that? But though I would do as much justice to the qualities of our countrymen as any gentleman in this House, though I may not indulge in high-flown and far-fetched expressions with respect to them like those we have listened to—for the people may have their parasites as well as monarchs and aristocracies—yet I have no doubt that, whatever may be their high qualities, our countrymen are subject to the same political laws that affect the condition of all other communities and nations. If you establish a democracy, you must in due season reap the fruits of a democracy. You will in due season have great impatience of public burdens combined in due season with great increase in the public expenditure. You will in due season reap the fruits of such united influence. You will in due season have wars entered into from passion, and not from reason; and you will in due season submit to peace ignominiously sought and ignominiously obtained, which will diminish your authority and perhaps endanger your independence. You will, in due season, with a democracy find that your property is less valuable and that your freedom is less complete. . . . That being my opinion, I cannot look upon what is called reduction of the franchise in boroughs but with alarm; and I have never yet met any argument which fairly encounters the objections that are urged to it. You cannot encounter it by sentimental assertions of the good qualities of the working classes. The greater their good qualities, the greater the danger. If you lay down as a principle that they are to enter the constituent body, not as individuals, but as a multitude, they must be the predominant class from their number; and if you dwell on their intelligence, you only increase the power they will exercise.

(iii) *Disraeli and Electoral Reform,* 1867

By the Reform Act of 1867, a Conservative Government doubled the parliamentary constituency by adding about a million new voters. The " line of political empiricism " which enfranchised ten-pound householders in towns in 1832 was abandoned in favour of rating household suffrage. In fact, after all Disraeli's insistence upon the traditional Conservative principle of enfranchising interests rather than numbers, on weighing votes rather than counting them, on quality rather than quantity, the Reform Act of 1867 instituted the principle of *numerical* democracy. In 1867, Disraeli abandoned the policy of enfranchising a " Praetorian Guard " of the working class; he abandoned "fancy franchises"; he abandoned everything in favour of what he called "a principle that is not liable to alteration". His defence was that a mere monetary lowering of the qualification could have been no more than a make-shift on the way to universal suffrage: Coleridge, Peel, and Wellington had all seen this in 1832, when they denounced the ten-pound suffrage as empirical trifling.

Whatever one may think of Disraeli's explanation of his action in 1867, the fact remains that Conservatism had accepted the democracy of numbers once and for all. The party of Pitt, Liverpool and Peel had shown that while it revered our ancient institutions it did not distrust the people. And the people, even if they said "Thank you, Mr Gladstone" for Disraeli's Act by voting the Liberals into power with a large majority in 1868, were soon to show that they did not distrust the Conservative Party. After the Liberal defeat in 1874, the Conservatives were in power for twenty-two out of the next thirty years. Thus the Liberal claim to the monopoly of reform was broken, Conservatism had taken the initiative, and the party could once more regard itself as a national institution.

The following passages are taken from Disraeli's speech on the third reading of the Reform Bill of 1867. The paragraphs have been rearranged slightly.

I have always said that the question of Parliamentary Reform was one which it was quite open to the Conservative Party to deal with. . . .

When we acceded to office, and to office for the first time, in the year 1852 . . . Mr. Hume brought forward . . . the whole question of Parliamentary Reform. . . . I expressed our opinion that if the subject were again opened—and its immediate re-opening we deprecated —the fault which had been committed in 1832 in neglecting to give a due share of the representation to the working classes ought to be remedied. . . . And I then contended, as I have done since, that before the settlement of 1832 franchises existed which were peculiar to the working classes, and that although the precise character of those franchises could not, perhaps, have been entirely defended, they should certainly not have been destroyed without the invention of fresh franchises more adapted to the times in which we live, and to the requirements of the classes concerned. . . .

The working classes will now probably have a more extensive sympathy with our political institutions, which, if they are in a healthy state, ought to enlist popular feeling because they should be embodiments of the popular requirements of the country.

It appeared to us that if this great change were made in the constitutional body there would be a better chance of arriving at the more patriotic and national feelings of the country than by admitting only a favoured section, who, in consideration of the manner in which they were treated, and the spirit in which they were addressed, together with the peculiar qualities which were ascribed to them, would regard themselves as marked out, as it were, from the rest of their brethren and the country, and as raised up to be critics rather than supporters of the Constitution . . . we still adhered to the policy of 1859, and believed that if you reduced the borough qualification—and some reduction was now inevitable—there was no resting-place until you came to a rating household suffrage. . . .

The question, therefore, for us practically to consider was—whether we were to accept this settlement of the borough franchise [i.e. as proposed by the Opposition] we will say at £5, or whether we should adhere to the conviction at which we had arrived in 1859, namely, that if you reduced the qualification there was no safe resting-place until you came to a household rating suffrage? . . . I think that the danger [i.e. of the latter] would be less, that the feeling of the large number would be more national than by admitting what I call the Praetorian Guard, a sort of class set aside, invested with peculiar privileges, looking with suspicion upon their superiors, and with disdain on those beneath them, with no friendly feelings towards the institutions of their country and with great confidence in themselves. I think you would have a better chance of touching the popular heart, of evoking the national sentiment, by embracing the great body of those men who occupy houses and fulfil the duties of citizenship by the payment of rates, than by the more limited and, in our opinion, more dangerous proposal. . . .

For my part, I do not believe that the country is in danger. I think England is safe in the race of men who inhabit her; that she is safe in something much more precious than her accumulated capital — her accumulated experience; she is safe in her national character, in her fame, in the traditions of a thousand years, and in that glorious future which I believe awaits her.

(iv) *The End of a Monopoly*

In a speech at the Mansion House Banquet in 1867, Disraeli rejoiced that the Tory Party could once more regard itself as the national party, and that the Liberal monopoly of reform was broken.

I have seen in my time several monopolies terminated, and recently I have seen the termination of the monopoly of Liberalism. Nor are we to be surprised when we see that certain persons who believed that they had an hereditary right, whenever it was necessary, to renovate the institutions of their country, should be somewhat displeased that any other persons should presume to interfere with those changes which, I hope in the spirit of true patriotism, they believed the requirements of the State rendered necessary. But I am sure that when the hubbub has subsided, when the shrieks and screams which were heard some time ago, and which have already subsided into sobs and sighs, shall be thoroughly appeased, nothing more terrible will be discovered to have occurred than that the Tory party has resumed its natural functions in the government of the country. For what is the Tory party unless it represents national feeling? If it do not represent national feeling, Toryism is nothing. It does not depend upon hereditary coteries of exclusive nobles. It does not attempt power by attracting to itself the spurious force which may accidentally arise from advocating cosmopolitan principles or talking cosmopolitan jargon. The Tory party is nothing unless it represent and uphold the institutions of the country. . . . I cannot help believing that, because my Lord Derby and his colleagues have taken a happy opportunity to enlarge the privilege of the people of England, we have not done anything but strengthen the institutions of the country, the essence of whose force is that they represent the interests and guard the rights of the people.

CHAPTER 4

ECONOMIC CHANGE:

(I) THE ECLIPSE OF THE LANDED INTEREST: CHANGING VALUES

Conservatism has always been closely associated with the interests, and—more important—with the moral and social values of the landed community. Conservatism believes in Country, and those who till the soil are, as Coleridge emphasised, naturally identified with the abiding purposes of the nation. Conservatism believes in organic change, thus preserving, as Burke put it, " the method of nature in the conduct of the state "; and those who till the soil can live only by observing the laws of nature—by respect for tradition and the health of the land. Conservatism believes in a balanced community in which no one interest is sacrificed to another and on the whole those who till the soil have upheld the claims of agriculture as an integral and wholesome part of the national interest rather than as a monopoly of all that is wise and worthwhile in the national life.

The story of the Conservative tradition, in respect of the movement of change which has turned England from a pre-dominantly agricultural to a predominantly industrial and commercial community, is one of wise if regretful concession: the counterpart of the story which we have seen under its political aspect in the preceding chapters. It has upheld the claims of agriculture, first to preponderance (not predominance) in a society preponderantly agricultural (and England was so at least down to the 1830's); then to fair treatment in relation to other elements in the nation's economic life; and finally, it has, with the passing away of a preponderantly rural England, kept before the nation both the moral and the utilitarian importance of a balanced economy.

(i) *What is the Landed Interest?*

Politically, in school text-books, "the Landed Interest" is generally taken to mean a group of selfish, reactionary, enclosing landlords, mostly titled, exclusively attached to fox-hunting, man-traps, and Corn Laws. In fact, it is the whole rural population, all who have to do with the cultivation of the soil and the multifarious industries dependent upon agriculture. According to the Census of 1831, these people made up more than half the population: not until 1851 were the scales balanced evenly between town and country people. The representative Englishman of the first half of the nineteenth century was rather William Cobbett than Francis Place.

Of the two passages that follow, the first is from a speech by Disraeli at Shrewsbury, on May 9, 1843. In it, he gives the widest possible content to the "landed interest"—including within it the estate of the Church and the "judicial fabric". The second passage, from Coleridge's *Church and State* (1830), illustrates the awareness of a critical Conservative of the way in which a small section of the Landed Interest, the great landowners, had come to sacrifice the interest of the whole to their own "imagined interests".

Gentlemen, when I talk of the preponderance of the landed interest, do not for a moment suppose that I mean merely the preponderance of " squires of high degree", that I am, in fact, thinking only of justices of the peace. My thought wanders further than a lordly tower or a manorial hall. I am looking in that phrase, in using that very phrase, to what I consider the vast majority of the English nation. I do not undervalue the mere superiority of the landed classes; on the contrary I think it a most necessary element of political power and national civilization; but I am looking to the population of our innumerable villages, to the crowds in our rural towns: aye, and I mean even something more than that by the landed interest—I mean that estate of the poor. . . . I mean by the estate of the poor, the great estate of the Church, which has, before this time, secured our liberty, and may, for aught I know, still secure our civilization. I mean also by the landed interest that great judicial fabric, that great building up of our laws and manners which is, in fact, the ancient polity of our Realm—those ancient institutions which we Conservatives are bound to uphold.

[I ask] whether the same causes which have deranged the equilibrium of the Landed and the Monied Interests in the Legislature, have not likewise deranged the balance between the two unequal divisions of the Landed Interest itself, viz., the Major Barons, or great Landowners, with or without title, and the great body of the Agricultural Community . . . thus giving to the real or imagined interests of the comparatively few the imposing name of the Interest of the whole—the Landed Interest! . . . [These] are questions to which the obdurate adherence to the jail-crowding Game Laws [and] the Corn Laws . . . may seem at a first view to suggest an answer in the affirmative. . . .

(ii) *Rural values:* (1) *The Individual*

William Cobbett was a Radical for Parliamentary Reform, but in all his social values he was a Tory of the deepest dye. His account of his own childhood and youth in rural England; his determination to bring up his own sons in the same way; and his life-long championship of the morality and wisdom of rural folk: these may be found in *The Progress of a Ploughboy to a Seat in Parliament,* edited by William Reitzel (Faber Library, No. 26, 1933). The following passages are taken from that text.

I was bred at the plough-tail, and in the Hop-Gardens of Farnham in Surrey, my native place, and which spot, as it so happened, is the neatest in England, and, I believe, in the whole world. All there is a garden. . . .

I was brought up under a father whose talk was chiefly about his garden and his fields, with regard to which he was famed for his skill and his exemplary neatness. From my very infancy, from the age of six years, when I climbed up the side of a steep sand rock, and there scooped me out a plot four feet square to make me a garden, and the soil for which I carried up in the bosom of my little blue smock-frock, I have never lost one particle of my passion for these healthy and rational and heart-cheering pursuits, in which every day presents something new, in which the spirits are never suffered to flag, and in which industry, skill and care are sure to meet with their due reward. I have never, for any eight months together, during my whole life, been without a garden. . . .

If the cultivators of the land be not, generally speaking, the most virtuous and most happy of mankind, there must be something at work in the community to counteract the operations of nature. This way of life gives the best security for health and strength of body. It does not teach, it necessarily produces early rising; constant forethought; constant attention; and constant care of dumb animals. The nature and qualities of all living things are known to country boys better than to philosophers. The seasons, the weather, the causes and effects of propagation, in cultivation, in tillage, are all known from habit, from incessant repetition of observation. The nature, the properties, the various uses, of different soils and woods are familiar to the mind of country boys. Riding, climbing, swimming, nothing comes amiss, and they are come, and are not sought. Rural affairs leave not a day, not an hour, unoccupied and without its cares, its promises, and its fruitions. The seasons, which wait for no man; the weather,

which is no respecter of persons, and which will be
what it will be, produce an habitual looking forward,
and make the farmer provident, whatever might have
been his natural disposition. The farmer's cares are
pleasing cares. His misfortunes can seldom be more
than lessons.

(iii) *Rural values:* (2) *The Village Community*

The Earl of Portsmouth, himself a landowner and a farmer,
broadcast two talks on rural England and its problems in July
and August 1947: they were reprinted in the *Listener,* July 31
and August 7. In his second talk, Lord Portsmouth stated the
moral case for the village community based on good husbandry
in terms which sum up the traditional Conservative attitude
without its too frequent accompaniment of sentimental idealism.
This passage is taken from that talk.

What I would like to bring to mind is that, from
Anglo-Saxon times, it was the individual village, de-
centralised for nearly every purpose, that had so much
to do in moulding institutions, forming the English sense
of independence and self-reliance; indeed, this helped
to give the Englishman his capacity in times of stress
and disaster to work in close loyalty and self-help with
his neighbour. Until very recently our towns were small
and our villages multitudinous and much more
populated.

This all meant that two hundred years ago, and
much later in many places, countrymen of all classes
were intensely conscious of their responsibilities and
aware of their personal standing and individuality.
Not all the bad times and changes at the turn of the
eighteenth century, nor all the *laissez-faire* and in-
dustrialism of the nineteenth, could really obliterate
their characteristic self-certainty. In a village fuel-
shortage, for instance, no one would have required

propaganda by every aid of press, poster and ether to make them save fuel. In a catchy harvest no one would have needed posters about "work or want" to get the harvest in. London was only one of a thousand capitals of England as far as human courage, leadership, skill, craftsmanship and responsibility were concerned. These villages very rarely grew up for one purpose or one industry alone. Even where, say, cottage weaving was the main occupation, the land and its cultivation, with its ancillary crafts, were always in the background. Cultivation of the land, in its original sense, meant worship as well as tillage, as witness the Latin verb *colere*. Tilling the soil, and all that went with it, was a matter of deeply serious care and reverence.

(iv) *Rural values:* (3) *The State*

Traditionally, the landed interest, great and small, has been attached by both interest and instinct to what Coleridge called the "permanence" of the state. Disraeli pointed out that the ancient English constitution was, in any case, a territorial constitution, and that neighbourhood, and neighbourly ways of doing things, were the best safeguards against the undermining of liberty by centralised government. Cobbett continually warned his day and generation against the tendency of war, and war-taxation, to destroy the "natural magistracy" of England and make everything dependent on central government.

I. COLERIDGE

Coleridge identified the landed interest with the permanence of the state, by which he meant the maintenance of its ancient institutions, rights, customs, manners and privileges. This was worked out in the second chapter of his book, *On the Constitution of the Church and State* (1830), although we find him asking as early as 1800: "Has not the hereditary possession of a landed estate been proved by experience to generate dispositions equally favourable to loyalty and established freedom?" The first paragraph below is taken from his *Second Lay Sermon* (1817), the rest from *Church and State*, Chapter II.

As the specific ends of agriculture are the maintenance, strength and security of the State, so . . . must its ultimate ends be the same as those of the State: even as the ultimate end of the spring and wheels of a watch must be the same as that of a watch. . . .

It will not be necessary to enumerate the several causes that combine to connect the permanence of a state with the land and the landed property. To found a family, and to convert his wealth into land, are twin thoughts, births of the same moment, in the mind of the opulent merchant when he thinks of reposing from his labours. From the class of the *Novi Homines* he redeems himself by becoming the staple ring of the chain by which the present will become connected with the past; and the tests and evidency of permanence afforded. To the same principle appertain primogeniture and hereditary titles, and the influence which these exert in accumulating large masses of property, and in counter-acting the antagonist and dispersive forces which the follies, the vices, and the misfortunes of individuals can scarcely fail to supply. To this, likewise, tends the proverbial obduracy of prejudices characteristic of the humbler tillers of the soil, and their aversion even to benefits that are offered in the form of innovations.

2. COBBETT

The emphasis which the Conservative tradition places upon locality, the neighbourhood, the primary associations of society, Burke's "little platoon", owes much to the implicit values of rural England. It finds explicit expression generally when it is threatened by encroachment at the hands of the centralising tendency of "the great State", a process that became increasingly evident during the Napoleonic War and in the period of Whig reformist rule that followed. It is best illustrated by the reaction of a countryman like Cobbett and a defender of the Landed Interest like Disraeli. The passage below is taken from Cobbett's *Political Register*, XLIV, December 21, 1822, and XXI, January 11, 1812.

I soon began to perceive that the fate of the Kingdom must finally turn upon what should be done with regard to the accursed thing called the National Debt. I saw the purpose for which it had been founded; I saw how completely it had answered that purpose; I saw how it had been the instrument of putting unbounded power into the hands of the Government; I saw how it had drawn the wealth of the country into masses, how it had destroyed the lower and middle classes of farmers, how it had added to the list of paupers, how it had beggared and degraded the country. . . .

In these years [i.e. during the war] the reputation of party was wholly destroyed. The people became weary of the thing. They saw that no change of men did them any good. . . . If there had been any great body of the nobility and gentry standing forward for a reform of the system, the spirit of the country would have been very different from what it was; but we saw no such body. The gentlemen of England seemed to have given up the country to the Minister of the day. Each seemed to care for nobody but himself ; and to think himself pretty well off if he had weight enough left to secure him the permission to have a sufficiency to live upon. The barriers erected by the pride and circumstance of family worth and by the circles of hospitality, were all swept away. There was no longer any intermediate link. The natural magistracy, as Hume calls it, was extinguished. All authority proceeded immediately from the government. There was not a village in England where the Surveyor of Taxes was not a more powerful man than the Lord of the Manor. The principle of obedience was that of fear and not of love.

3. DISRAELI

Disraeli's views on the " territorial constitution " are illustrated in Section ii (1) of the following chapter, where the following passage will be found in its context.

. . . In England we have a territorial constitution. We have thrown upon the land the revenues of the Church, the administration of justice, and the estate of the poor: and this has been done not to gratify the pride or pamper the luxury of the proprietors of the land, but because in a territorial constitution you, and those whom you have succeeded, have found the only security for self-government, the only barrier against that centralising system which has taken root in other countries.

(v) *The Landed Interest infected with the Spirit of Trade*

Only on the assumption that land bore special and peculiar burdens in the public interest could the protection of the landed interest by Corn Laws be justly maintained in an England whose manufactures were being exposed to foreign competition by the policies of Huskisson and Peel.

The infection of the landed interest with the spirit of trade—a process noticeable in the sixteenth century, and increasing ever since—enhanced by the temptation to make quick profits when agricultural prices were high during war years, and by the sheer pressure of war-taxes on the farmer: this process had the inevitable consequence of exposing the landed interest to the accusation of being simply a commercial affair, liable to be treated on the same footing as cotton-spinning, or any other industry. Land forfeited its special claims to protection because it forgot, or was deprived of, its special responsibilities.

I. COLERIDGE

Coleridge's *Second Lay Sermon* (1817) is much concerned with this change. The whole of the following passage is taken from that source, with the exception of the second paragraph, which is interpolated from " Table Talk ", March 31, 1833.

It was one among the many anomalies of the late war that it acted, after a few years, as a universal stimulant. We almost monopolised the commerce of the world. The high wages of our artisans and the high prices of agricultural produce intercirculated. Leases of unusual length not seldom enabled the provident and thrifty farmer to purchase the estate he had rented. . . . I leave to your own experience and recollection the assemblage of folly, presumption and extravagance that followed in the procession of our late unprecedented prosperity; and the blind practices and blending passions of speculation in the commercial world, with the shoal of ostentatious fooleries and sensual vices which the sudden influx of wealth let in on our farmers and yeomanry. . . .

That agriculture requires principles essentially different from those of trade; that a gentleman ought not to regard his estate as a merchant his cargo or a shopkeeper his stock—admits of an easy proof from the purposes of agriculture itself, which ultimately are the same as those of the state of which it is the offspring. . . .

Nothing but the most horrible perversion of humanity and moral justice, under the specious name of political economy, could have blinded men to this truth as to the possession of land—the law of God having connected indissolubly the cultivation of every rood of earth with the maintenance and watchful labour of man. But money, stock, riches by credit, transferable and convertible at will, are under no such obligations; and, unhappily, it is from the selfish, autocratic possession of *such* property, that our land-owners have learnt their present theory of trading with that which was never meant to be an object of commerce. . . .

Two objects only can be proposed in the management of an estate considered as stock in trade—first, that the returns shall be the largest, quickest and securest possible; and secondly, with the least outgoings in the providing, over-looking and collecting the same. . . . Am I disposing of a bale of goods? . . . The personal worth of those whom I benefit in the course of the process, or whether the persons are really benefited or no, is no concern of mine. The market and the shop are open to all. To introduce any other principle into trade but that of obtaining the highest price with adequate security for articles fairly described would be tantamount to the position that trade ought not to exist.

If this be admitted, then what as a tradesman I cannot do, it cannot be my duty as a tradesman to attempt. . . . If my estate be such, my plan must be to make the most of it, as I would of any other mode of capital. As my rents will ultimately depend on the quantity and value of the produce raised and brought into the best market from my land, I will entrust the latter to those who, bidding the most, have the largest capital to employ on it: and this I cannot effect but by dividing it into the fewest tenures, as none but extensive farms will be an object to men of extensive capital and enterprising minds. I must prefer this system likewise for my own ease and security. The farmer is of course actuated by the same motives as the landlord: and, provided they are both faithful to their engagements, the objects of both will be: 1, the utmost produce that can be raised without injuring the estate; 2, the least possible consumption of the produce on the estate itself ; 3, at the lowest wages; and 4, with the substitution of machinery for human labour wherever the former will cost less and do the same work. . . .

It would border on an affront to the understandings of the members of our Landed Interest were I to explain in detail what the plan and conduct of a gentleman would be, if, as a result of his own free conviction the marketable produce of his estates were made a subordinate consideration to the living and moral growth that is to remain on the land. . . .

(vi) *The Landed Interest infected with the Spirit of Trade*

2. COBBETT

The first of the following passages supplies a concrete instance, in Cobbett's vivid style, of the " ostentatious fooleries and sensual vices which ", as Coleridge asserted, " the sudden influx of wealth let in on our farmers and yeomanry ". It is taken from *Rural Rides* (Everyman Edition, Vol. I, p. 250 ff). Carpets, bell-pulls, mahogany and parlours were Cobbett's idea of fooleries in farmhouses. The remainder is made up of passages from *The Progress of a Ploughboy*, pp. 100, 245 and 274: but similar castigation of the new rich owners of the land might be found almost anywhere in Cobbett's writing.

I went . . . to a sale at a farm where a farmer was quitting. Here I had a view of what had long been going on all over the country. . . . Everything about this farmhouse was formerly the scene of plain manners and plentiful living. Oak clothes-chests, oak bedsteads, oak chest of drawers, and oak tables to eat on, long, strong, and well supplied with joint stools. Some of the things were many hundreds of years old. But all appeared to be in a state of decay and nearly of disuse. There appeared to have been hardly any family in that house, where formerly there had been, in all probability, from ten to fifteen men, boys and maids: and, which was the worst of all, there was a parlour! Aye, and a carpet and bell-pull, too! One end of the front of this once plain and substantial house had been moulded into a " parlour "; and there was a mahogany table, and the fine chairs, and the fine glass, and all as bare-faced upstart as any stock-jobber in the kingdom could boast of. And I daresay it had been *Squire* Charrington and the *Miss* Charringtons; and not plain Master Charrington and his son Hodge and his daughter Betty Charrington, all of whom the accursed system had, in all likelihood, transmuted into a species of mock gentlefolk.

The funding system was eating the heart out of the nobility; stifling every high and honourable feeling. It was engaged in a desperate contest against the aristocracy and monarchy of England, and this contest must terminate in the destruction of one or the other. . . . It was impossible to look, without indignation, at the group who wielded the destinies of England; who, amidst a mass of blunders that covered a country with misery, sat, perked up like schoolmasters and their ushers, while the owners of the soil, the natural magistracy of the country, the guardians of its happiness and its honour, stood before them like a set of schoolboys, silently listening to their pompous imbecility, and patiently waiting for their fate at their hands. . . . It was easy, after this, to see in what the present Lords differed from the Lords of former times.

In everything; except in the shape of their bodies. It had been the business of the Lords, each one to protect his people from wrong; to see that they had fair play; they were their advocates in courts of justice. The bishops and abbots were in Parliament to take care that the poor were not plundered out of their patrimony; and thus nobility was " the cheap defence of the realm ". What do we behold now? a prodigious band of spungers, living upon the labour of the industrious part of the community.

ECONOMIC CHANGE: (II) THE ECLIPSE OF THE LANDED INTEREST: REPEAL OF THE CORN LAWS, AND AFTER

The repeal of the Corn Laws, in 1846, is of importance in the history of the Conservative tradition for two reasons.

In the first place, the struggle elicited from Disraeli a fairly complete statement of the perennial Conservative attitude towards the Landed Interest, its social significance, its claims, and its obligations. Although it was no longer possible to uphold convincingly many of the claims which Disraeli asserted, there is a residual interest in them that is worthy of remembrance in any society which values the continuity of its institutions.

Secondly, in repealing the Corn Laws, Peel professed to act as a true Conservative. He split his party. Conservatism was, as Disraeli said, a corpse for the next twenty years. Yet, by basing himself on what he rightly conceived to be the national, as distinct from a sectional, interest, Peel established a claim for Conservatism upon the future gratitude of the nation which was to be met a hundredfold.

By 1850, Disraeli himself was to declare that Protection was not only dead but buried. Peel may have been wrong in his timing. He was certainly at fault in his leadership of his party. But his action in 1846 is the most striking, even if the most clumsy, example of that political empiricism which Burke held to be the whole art of statesmanship. It was a perfectly sincere and public-spirited example of that preference for practice over doctrine which we associate with the Aristotelian tradition of Conservatism in all ages.

(i) *The Corn Laws defended by Peel*

The speech from which this passage is taken was delivered by Peel in a debate in the House of Commons on a Petition,

March 19, 1834. He here makes it clear that he was aware of the importance of accompanying any reduction of the duties on corn with a corresponding reform of local taxation: he merely touches upon the moral and social considerations involved.

Before you determine to take off the restriction on the import of foreign corn, you ought first to look at the burdens to which the landholder is subject, and at the difference in degree in which those burdens, whether they be local or public burdens, press upon the landed proprietor and the manufacturer respectively. Consider the land-tax, the malt-tax, and the payment of tithes. . . . The total amount of the poor-rates paid in the year 1823, in England and Wales, was £6,703,000. Of this, dwelling-houses paid £1,762,000; the land £4,602,000; the mills and factories only £247,000,—namely, one eighteenth part of the payment of the land. I ask, therefore, can it be said, after such a statement, that the local burdens are fairly appropriated between the landed and the manufacturing interests? —and have not the proprietors of land a right to claim, on this head alone, that degree of protection for their property which is equivalent to the excess of contribution to which the land is subject? I will put out of the question the policy of supporting the landed interest on grounds involving moral and social considerations. I will not dwell upon the importance, in a national point of view, of encouraging the improvement of the land, or the effect which that improvement has had in promoting the general health and diminishing the average mortality of the country. I will not now discuss whether there be not other and higher considerations for a great country than the mere accumulation of wealth, and whether we should be a happier, even if we were a richer people, if this country presented nothing but vast congregations of steam-engines and factories separated by morasses and rabbit warrens. I will, I say, put all considerations of this kind out of the question, and merely ask, is it fair or just to hold up the landed proprietor as a monopolist claiming an exclusive protection for his property from motives of mere pecuniary gain? If there be a free trade in corn, is it not evident that the landholder will be no longer able to bear those burdens that press peculiarly on the land? Let not the manufacturer suppose, that if the interest of the landholder is sacrificed, he can bear his present burdens;—there must be a different appropriation of those burdens—a transfer of them from the landed to more prosperous interests.

(ii) *The Corn Laws defended by Disraeli*

Putting aside the personal equation of his relations with Peel, and the ambitions of a rising politician, Disraeli defended the Corn Laws on three grounds: (1) the importance of safeguarding the Landed Interest under a territorial constitution: to maintain the preponderance of the Landed Interest was to safeguard locality (and freedom) against centrality (and bureaucratic despotism); (2) the importance of maintaining a *balance* of interests: to prevent the shifting of the balance of power from a responsible aristocracy to an irresponsible manufacturing middle class; and (3) to do justice to that section of the community which bore the greatest financial burdens—particularly in the form of rates.

Much of what he said and wrote at this time was already anachronistic, but it is important in the history of the Conservative tradition for the perpetuation of ideas which survive the situation and circumstances that gave birth to their expression. The principal ideas which remain important within the body of Conservative thought are two: the responsibilities of property, and the value of local self-agency.

I. THE TERRITORIAL CONSTITUTION

This passage, from a speech delivered in the House of Commons on Mr. Miles's Amendment, on February 20, 1846, is the most important example of Disraeli's stress on the constitutional importance of the Landed Interest.

I believe that there are burdens, heavy burdens, on the land; but the land has great honours, and he who has great honours must have great burdens. But I wish them to bear in mind that their cause must be sustained by great principles. I venture feebly and slightly to indicate those principles, principles of high policy, on which their system ought to be sustained. First, without reference to England, looking at all countries, I say that it is the first duty of the Minister and the first interest of the State to maintain a balance between the two great branches of national industry. . . . Why we should maintain that balance . . . involves political considerations, social considerations, affecting the happiness, prosperity, and morality of the people, as well as the stability of the State. But I go further; I say that in England we are bound to do more. I repeat what I have repeated before, that in this country there are special reasons why we should not only maintain the balance . . . but why we should give a preponderance —I do not say a predominance—to the agricultural branch; and the reason is, because in England we have a territorial constitution. We have thrown upon the land the revenues of the Church, the administration of justice, and the estate of the poor: and this has been done not to gratify the pride or pamper the luxury of the proprietors of the land, but because in a territorial constitution you, and those whom you have succeeded, have found the only security for self-government, the only barrier against that centralising system which has

taken root in other countries. I have always maintained
these opinions. My constituents are not landlords; they
are not aristocrats; they are not great capitalists; they
are the children of industry and toil, and they believe,
first, that their material interests are involved in a
system which favours native industry, by ensuring at
the same time real competition, but they also believe
that their political and social interests are involved in
a system by which their rights and liberties have been
guaranteed: and I agree with them—I have the same
old-fashioned notions.

2. THE CLASS-ISSUE

Disraeli brought the charge of class-government, or the
middle-class monopoly of power, in a speech on the Income Tax,
March 1848.

Have we not heard it stated before, by no less a
person than the honourable member for Manchester
[Mr. Cobden] that the gentlemen opposite to me are
a middle-class government—that they look to the
middle class for power, and the middle class look to
them for their advantages? A few years ago, was it
not held out as the greatest opprobrium that the
agricultural interest was supported by class legislation?
Were we not told, on every opportunity, in every
manner, that class legislation was the great evil of the
country? But now that they have obtained their ends,
now that they have passed their measures; now that
their beautiful commercial system is working its results;
now that they think they have confirmed themselves
in political authority and parliamentary power, they
have the unblushing front to say the Government shall
be a middle-class Government and shall work solely for
the middle classes. Sir, I do not believe that, after all

that has occurred, gentlemen here will submit without a struggle to this. No, Sir; if we have thought it wise to terminate those commercial distinctions which are supposed—I think erroneously—to have affected our social condition, it will be but a poor consolation for us to discover that the only return we have for a diminished revenue and a declining commerce is the arrogant authority of a class who obtained power by false pretences, and now, possessing it, attempt to exercise it merely for their own advantage.

3. THE LANDED INTEREST MALIGNED AND FLEECED

In a speech in the House of Commons on Local Taxation, in March 1849, Disraeli voiced the resentment of the Landed Interest at what it felt to be the partial and unfair treatment of its claims by the Legislature. Disraeli sums up the value of the territorial principle in the constitution and the element of stability which that Interest affords to a well-governed state, and concludes with an appeal for partnership between the rival interests.

The complainants are those various classes that, combined and united, form what is called in popular language "the landed interest"; a portion of the nation which, whether we look at their property or their numbers, or the weight and influence which necessarily result from their social position and their interesting occupation, may still be accounted the most considerable order in our society. . . .

They have witnessed the rise and development in this country of new properties, of new species of influence; and they have witnessed them without jealousy, because it is part of their commercial creed that prosperity depends upon the union of classes. They have witnessed without any hostile feelings the right and rightful representation of those new interests and properties in this House since its reconstruction.

But though they have observed these great incidents
with no other feeling than such as becomes a manly
mind, it is but right that you should understand that it
is not without emotion they have observed that the
whole course of your legislation for years has been to
invest those new properties and interests with privileges,
and simultaneously to deprive them of theirs. . . . They
have not forgotten that their noble industry, which in
the old days was considered the invention of gods and
the occupation of heroes, has been stigmatised and
denounced as an incubus upon English enterprise. They
have not forgotten that even the very empire that was
created by their valour and the devotion of their fathers
has been held up to public hatred, as a cumbersome
and ensanguined machine, only devised to pamper
the luxury and feed the rapacity of our territorial
houses. . . . I tell you and every member of the House,
every good and wise man must feel that nothing is to
be more deprecated, nothing is more dangerous, than
that considerable classes of the country should deem
that they are treated unfairly by the Legislature. Sir,
the spirit of the landed interest is deeply wounded.
Whether they have the foundation for this feeling or
not, it is one which I would recommend any minister
not to treat with contempt.

I fancy, Sir, it has been somewhat too long the
practice to believe that you might conduct yourselves
toward the landed interest with impunity. It was even
a proverb with Sir Robert Walpole that the landed
interest might be fleeced at pleasure; and I observe at
no time has that interest been more negligently treated
than when demagogues are denouncing it as an
oligarchical usurpation. But this may be dangerous
play if you are outraging justice. You think you may

trust their proverbial loyalty. Trust their loyalty, but do not abuse it. I dare say it may be said of them, as it was said 2,000 years ago, in the most precious legacy of political science that has descended to us . . . that the agricultural class is the least given to sedition. . . .

Your system and theirs are exactly contrary. They invite union. They believe that national prosperity can only be produced by the prosperity of all classes. You prefer to remain in isolated splendour and solitary magnificence. But believe me I speak not as your enemy when I say that it will be an exception to the principles which seem hitherto to have ruled society, if you can succeed in maintaining the success at which you aim without the possession of that permanence and stability which the territorial principle alone can afford.

Although you may for a moment flourish after their destruction—although your ports may be filled with shipping, your factories smoke on every plain—I see no reason why you should form an exception to that which the page of history has mournfully recorded; that you too should not fade like the Tyrian dye, and moulder like the Venetian palaces. But united with the land, you will obtain the best and surest foundation upon which to build your enduring welfare; you will find in that interest a counsellor in all your troubles, in danger your champion, and in adversity your steady customer. It is to assist in producing this result, Sir, that I am about to place these resolutions in your hands. I wish to see the agriculture, the commerce, and the manufactures of England, not adversaries but co-mates and partners—and rivals only in the ardour of their patriotism and in the activity of their public spirit.

(iii) *Peel defends Repeal*

Peel should be heard in his own defence not only of what he did, but of how he did it. The present section has been divided into two headings in order that he should be heard on both questions. They are equally important for the history of Conservatism: the first, for his claim to have acted in the best interests of the nation, the landed interest itself, and the constitution; the second, for his defence against the charge (see section (i) of this chapter) that he ran away with his party.

(a) PEEL'S DEFENCE OF WHAT HE DID

These passages are taken from his speech vindicating Repeal, in the House of Commons, May 15, 1846.

Sir, I have explained more than once what were the circumstances under which I felt it to be my duty to take this course. I did feel in November last that there was just cause for apprehension of scarcity and famine in Ireland. I am stating what were the apprehensions I felt at that time, what were the motives from which I acted; and those apprehensions, though they may be denied now, were at least shared then by those honourable gentlemen who sit below the gangway. . . .[1]
I may have been wrong, but my impression was, first, that my duty towards a country threatened with famine required that that which had been the ordinary remedy under all similar circumstances, should be resorted to, namely, that there should be free access to the food of man from whatever quarter it might come. I was prepared to give the best proof which public men generally can give of the sincerity of their opinions, by tendering my resignation of office, and devolving upon others the duty of proposing this measure[2]; and,

---

[1] Seceding members of the Party.

[2] Peel had resigned the government on December 5, 1845; but Lord John Russell being unable to form an administration, he returned to office on December 20.

Sir, I felt this, that if these laws were once suspended, and there was unlimited access to food, the produce of other countries, I and those with whom I acted felt the strongest conviction that it was not for the interest of the agricultural party that an attempt should be made permanently to reimpose restrictions on the importation of food. . . .

Now, all of you admit that the real question at issue is the improvement of the social and moral condition of the masses of the population. We wish to elevate, in the gradation of society, that great class which gains its support by manual labour. That is agreed on all hands. The mere interest of the landlords, the mere interest of the occupying tenants, important as they are, are subordinate to the great question—what is calculated to increase the comforts, to improve the condition, and elevate the social character of the millions who subsist by manual labour, whether they are engaged in manufactures or in agriculture . . . I will not hesitate to say my firm belief is, that it is most consistent with prudence and good policy, most consistent with the real interests of the landed proprietors themselves, most consistent with the maintenance of a territorial aristocracy, seeing by how precarious a tenure, namely, the vicissitude of the seasons, you hold your present protective system; I say that it is my firm belief that it is for the advantage of all classes, in these times of comparative comfort and comparative calm, to anticipate the angry discussions which might arise, by proposing at once a final settlement of the question. . . .

I admit that I have defended the existence of the Corn Laws. . . . But, when I am told that I am acting inconsistently with the principles of my whole life by advocating free trade, I give this statement a peremptory denial. . . . Did I not declare that the principle of political economy suggested the purchasing in the cheapest and the selling in the dearest market? Did I not say that I thought there was nothing so special in the produce of agriculture that should exempt it from the application of this principle which we have applied already to other articles? You have a right, I admit, to taunt me with any change of opinion upon the Corn Laws; but when you say that by my adoption of the principle of free trade I have acted in contradiction to those principles which I have always avowed during my whole life, that charge, at least, I say, is destitute of foundation. . . .

I always will assert the right to give that advice which I conscientiously believe to be conducive to the general well-being. I was not considering . . . what was the best bargain to make for a party. I was considering first what were the best measures to avert a great calamity and, as a secondary consideration, to relieve that interest, which I was bound to protect, from the odium of refusing to acquiesce in measures which I thought to be necessary for the purpose of averting that calamity. Sir, I cannot charge myself or my colleagues with having been unfaithful to the trust committed to us. I do not believe that the great institutions of this country have suffered during our administration of power. . . .

Sir, if I look to the prerogatives of the Crown, if I look to the position of the Church, if I look to the influence of the aristocracy, I cannot charge myself with having taken any course inconsistent with Conservative principles, calculated to endanger the privileges of any branch of the Legislature, or any institutions of the country. My earnest wish has been, during my tenure of power, to impress the people of this country with a belief that the Legislature was animated by a sincere desire to frame its legislation upon the principles of equity and justice. I have a strong belief that the greatest object which we or any other Government can contemplate should be to elevate the condition of that class of the people with whom we are brought into no direct relationship by the exercise of the elective franchise. I wish to convince them that our object has been to apportion taxation, that we shall relieve industry and labour from any undue burden, and transfer it, so far as is consistent with the public good, to those who are better enabled to bear it. . . .

Deprive me of power to-morrow, you can never deprive me of the consciousness that I have exercised the powers committed to me from no corrupt or interested motives, from no desire to gratify ambition or attain any personal object; that I have laboured . . . to increase the confidence of the great body of the people in the justice of your decisions, and by the means of equal law to dispense with all coercive powers, to maintain loyalty to the Throne and attachment to the Constitution, from a conviction of the benefit that will accrue to the great body of the people.

(b) PEEL'S DEFENCE OF HOW HE DID IT

Peel's self-justification against the points raised in criticism of his conduct of affairs in 1845–46 brings out at almost every turn the traditional Conservative notions of government and its responsibilities.

1. THAT REPEAL SHOULD HAVE BEEN PUT TO THE ELECTORATE

Peel replies to this point in his *Memoirs* (ed. by Mahon and Cardwell, 1856, Vol. II, p. 166). His reply is wholly consistent with the truly Conservative conception of Parliament as a free, dispassionate and deliberative body, which was illustrated in Chapter 1 of Part II, above.

It appeared to me . . . that there were grave objections to the proposal that we should notify to the constituent body on the eve of a General Election the intention to repeal the Corn Laws for the express purpose of inviting an expression of their opinion on that particular subject. I thought such an appeal would ensure a bitter conflict between different classes of society, and would preclude the possibility of dispassionate consideration by a Parliament, the members of which would have probably committed themselves by explicit declarations and pledges, and would approach a discussion which could not be deferred, with all the heat and animosity engendered by severe contests at the hustings.

2. THAT HE SHOULD HAVE TAKEN HIS PARTY MORE FULLY INTO HIS CONFIDENCE

There can be no doubt that in the crisis of the Corn Laws Peel was acting on a conception of the personal responsibility and initiative of the first Minister of the Crown that belonged to the century of Walpole and the Pitts rather than to the post-1832 era. His defence (*Memoirs*, Vol. II, pp. 319–321 and 322–324) is based on the plea of emergency, and the delicate position which existed inside the party.

There are, I know, many who have freely admitted that a Minister was fully justified in the adoption of the measures of 1846, and who do not blame the resolution taken, but consider that some better mode of giving effect to it might have been devised—who are of opinion that needless reserve was maintained towards a powerful party, and that a degree of irritation was thereby produced which more frank and unreserved communication would have prevented or mitigated.

I wish to give some explanation upon this point. I am the more desirous to give it because it was my intention—but for the unforeseen events of the autumn of 1845—to enter into that friendly communication, the omission of which is blamed and lamented, to apprise the Conservative Party, before the Corn Law could be discussed in the Session of 1846, that my views with regard to the policy of maintaining that law had undergone a change. . . . That unreserved communication which I had thus contemplated—which is possible and most desirable under ordinary circumstances—was in this case unfortunately precluded by the peculiar character of the unforeseen emergency for which it was necessary to provide, and the peculiar position of the Cabinet in respect of the measures to be adopted. . . . It was impossible to reconcile the repeal of the Corn Laws by me with the keeping together of the Conservative Party, and I had no hesitation in sacrificing the subordinate object, and with it my own political interests. It is a very difficult matter under any circumstances to convey information to a particular party as to the intention of a Minister in regard to questions which are intimately connected with great commercial speculations and great pecuniary gains and losses; it is ten times more difficult to make such a communication to a selected few. . . .

If, before announcing in the House of Commons my intention to repeal the Corn Laws, I had tried to gain acquiescence, either by belabouring individuals separately, or by summoning the party generally, I should have received scarcely one promise of support. I should have had on the part of the most moderate a formal protest against the course I intended to pursue; to the most violent I should have given facilities for organised opposition; I should have appeared to be flying in the face of a whole party, and contumaciously disregarding their opinions and advice after I had professed to consult them; but (what is of infinitely more importance) *I should have failed in carrying the repeal of the Corn Laws.*

Now, I was resolved *not to fail.* I did not fail; and if I had to fight the battle over again, I would fight it in the same way.

(iv) *Conservatism returns to its* moutons—*and corn*

Two world wars have made the English people land-conscious again in the best way possible—by making them food-conscious. Conservative thinkers, who have never departed from their traditions, find reason to take heart. Here is Mr. G. M. Young in his essay, " Ourselves " (Signpost Books, 1944).

There are many things in our favour. One is that millions of people who had never thought of it before, have come to see that the country is not something vaguely pretty from which Tory Squires chase a depressed proletariat with oaths and riding whips (a picture still current, I gather, in the U.S.A., and in the senior branches of the Labour Party at home): but is in very truth their own larder and their own dairy. They have learnt to shake their heads at a drought, to grin congratulations at one another when the rain comes, and to respect the energy and skill, thanks to which we are, in the fifth year of war, certainly the best fed people in Europe, and possibly in the world.

In the second place, we know incomparably more than we did even twenty years ago about food itself, its varieties and their special values. The Chief Housekeeper, looking along the family, can now make a pretty accurate judgment of what they need to keep them all in health and good humour. But to calculate how much she shall order from the Home Farm and how much she shall buy from the shops across the way, from the Dominions, from the United States, from the Argentine, it is a delicate and contentious business. A hundred years ago the argument was clear—we were the workshop of the world, we could buy all we wanted abroad, and our population was growing faster than we could feed it out of our own resources. That being so, the conclusion was unanswerable—open the ports to foreign grain. But to-day we are only one among many workshops, and our population, nearly stationary, may soon begin to decline. The conditions are inverted but our understanding of the problem is more intimate and thorough.

In other words, our agricultural policy should be grounded on a marriage between sound farming and healthy feeding. . . . We can see what the land has done for us and at least we can make sure that . . . we keep the land in good heart. We may need it all. Or we may find that some of it can be diverted to more useful purposes. . . . But . . . we should insist on this, that no land shall be taken from its primary and proper use without due consideration and public consent. . . . If any ghost of late Victorian Radicalism creeps out of his mausoleum at this point and gibbers about Landlordism and Nationalisation of the Land, he can gibber to himself. I shall not stay to listen, I have other things to think of : things—and people.

(v) *Husbandry and the Profit Motive*

Writing as a confessed townsman, Mr. Quintin Hogg, in his *Case for Conservatism* (1947), Chapter 21, re-states the natural

affinity between Conservatism and rural values. The strength
of the Conservative tradition in this matter could scarcely be
better illustrated than by comparing this passage with the
excerpts from Coleridge in Chapter 4 (v), above.

Agriculture was the occupation which to some extent
determined the attitude of Conservatives to industry
and indeed to politics in general. . . . It is an attitude
to the agricultural industry which explains and defines
more simply than in any other case the Conservative
approach to the profit motive.

Conservatives, as it is well known, have no fault to
find with the profit motive as such. All farming in this
country is carried on with a view to profit. But nevertheless it is a complete travesty of the Conservative
attitude to contend that profit is the sole governing
motive of which Conservatives approve in industry.
The farmer who farms *solely* with a view to profit is
not a good farmer. He impoverishes the land instead
of enriching it. The Conservative view of agriculture,
and of industry in general, whilst it does not discoun-
tenance profit, is based primarily on the theory of good
husbandry. It is the agriculture of traditional British
farming and not the bastard agriculture of the
American dust bowl which attracts Conservatives. . . .

When you go to a typical British farm to-day you
see the results not of the efforts of a good or a bad
farmer. . . . What you see is the concentrated result of
some twelve generations of good husbandry, the devoted
efforts which for over four centuries Englishmen have
lavished *on the land*. I emphasise the words *on the
land* because, although the farmers worked for profit
and the labourers for hire, neither the farmers nor the
labourers received the true reward of their efforts. The

real reward redounded to the benefit of England; not just of the Englishmen of that time, but of the Englishmen of a future time. They returned to the land in the form of manure, good drains, sound fences, and deeply cultivated fields more than they took out of it by way of sustenance for man and beast, until, strange to relate, the average yield per acre of wheat from an English field is vastly greater than that of the Canadian wheat-belt, and almost unsurpassed anywhere in the world.

That is good husbandry, and that is the fundamental attitude of the Conservative Party to farming and to industry for that matter. The profit motive is accepted and is used as the normal driving force, but it is not permitted to dominate, for if it does we shall do violence to the heritage which we have received from of old. . . .

The theory of *laissez-faire* . . . preached that in the long run it paid to buy in the cheapest and sell in the dearest market. It was cheaper to buy the products of those who raped the virgin prairie of America without restoring what they took out, and were thus busy in creating new deserts in a highly fertile land, than to buy the costly products of England's highly dunged and fertile fields, which would be handed on better and more beautiful than they had been inherited. Rather than pay wages which would have enabled the poor to buy British products, they gave them access to the markets of the world. . . .

The doctrine of buying in the cheapest and selling in the dearest market includes a great deal of truth. But it ignores the long-term welfare of the race—the land, the virility and health of a people, and the spiritual and religious values it deliberately excludes from policy. It is dust bowl farming—both literally and metaphorically — and the Conservative protests that unchecked it will produce a desert. . . .

The Conservative believes that farming is more than a business ; it is a way of life, essential for the well-being of the community in war and peace. . . . The Conservative believes—and so far science has borne him out—that a purely urban community tends to die out. That this is not wholly true is obvious from the survival of the Jews in spite of the absence of direct contact with the land for many centuries. But in the main Conservatives are justified in claiming that an agricultural population forms the best possible stock for maintaining a healthy breed of men.

(vi) *The Tradition and the Future*

Lord Portsmouth, in the broadcast talk already quoted (Part II, Chapter 4, iii), defined " rural revival " in both economic and spiritual terms. The following passages show the Conservative tradition at grips with this theme *vis-à-vis* the future.

I believe that only by alliance with nature can we achieve any harmony for ourselves or security for our children as families or as a community. . . . Also, by an accident of fate, I happen to be an owner of land as well as a farmer. As both, and perhaps especially as an owner, I regard myself as a trustee for the future of a small parcel of England and those who serve that parcel with me. So also I feel an immediate duty, as a farmer, to produce good crops and healthy stock. All this may sound self-righteous and perhaps even self-important, but I can assure you it is the feeling of all owners and tenant farmers worth their salt. But we really are not self-important because we know that the earth and those who serve her, whether it be ourselves or our neighbours, are measured by the quality of that service, and this makes us feel very small in the long cycle of events.

So I know, with these instincts pressing in on me, that England cannot be happy or healthy, or even secure, until she grows far more food than she does to-day and, by good husbandry, maintains and even increases the fertility of her soil. And I am equally certain that, no matter what machines may be invented, it will be enough men and women on the land and serving the living earth which alone can do the job properly, for the future and the present. And I am equally certain that there must be a proper balance between those who serve the soil and those who form the complex pattern of urban community and occupation. Hence human beings are the first crop on the land . . . men and women who really want to live there and to work there and whose children will find a wide variety of work and opportunity, bound by a common factor which is understanding of the rhythmic discipline of soil and season, which in turn brings care and craftsmanship to bear on whatever task may happen.

CHAPTER 6

ECONOMIC CHANGE:
(III) INDUSTRIALISM AND TORY DEMOCRACY

With the triumph of the manufacturing and commercial interest over the landed interest, signallised by such events as the passing of the Reform Bills and the Repeal of the Corn Laws, Conservatism took upon itself increasingly the function of reconciliation between classes in a society of increasingly bitter class warfare. With its traditional claims to be the national party, wedded to the interests of no single class of society (claims substantially strengthened by Peel, despite the charge of Disraeli and the Chartists, that the Corn Laws were repealed in the interests of the manufacturers), Conservatism could approach the urgent "Condition-of-England Problem" without sectional or doctrinal prejudice. The taint of *laissez-faire* doctrine, which embarrassed the humane and socially responsible Tories of the age of Pitt and Liverpool, was purged away by Tory humanitarians and philanthropists like Shaftesbury, Oastler and Sadler; by feudal aristocratic Tories like Lord John Manners, George Smythe, the young Disraeli, and "Young England" in general; and by Conservative prophets like Coleridge and Carlyle. The Tory name became associated with Factory Acts, legislation on behalf of Trade Unions, and finally with Education Acts.

Acting always upon empirical grounds of the social necessities of the moment, but with a firm grasp upon the principle of the primacy of the moral free-agency of the individual, Conservatism tended, as the situation of the working classes grew more desperate, to lay its stress on the constructive potentialities of the state. At the same time it went out to win the working-class electorate to Tory principles, in keeping with Disraeli's view, expressed in 1846 (see Chapter V (iv) (e), above), that the answer to the new thraldom of capital must be found in " the invigorating energies of an educated and enfranchised people ".

(i) " *Yorkshire Slavery* ": a Tory indictment

On October 16, 1830, there appeared in the *Leeds Mercury* what the latest biographer of Richard Oastler has justly described as " one of the most famous letters of the nineteenth century " (see *Tory Radical*, by Cecil Driver, 1940, Chapter IV.) Oastler was land-steward to a Yorkshire landlord; a Tory by instinct and conviction; and, early, an Evangelical Christian. An advocate of the emancipation of the negro slaves of the British Empire, he turned in pity and indignation to the problem of the white slaves of Huddersfield and Bradford. His series of letters on " Yorkshire Slavery " in the *Leeds Mercury*, and his great crusade for legislative intervention in the conditions of factory labour, rank him with Shaftesbury as one of the greatest makers of Tory reform politics of the nineteenth century.

The following passages are from the first and third of his series of " Letters ".

Gentlemen,—no heart responded with truer accents to the sounds of liberty which were heard in the Leeds Cloth-hall Yard, on the 22nd instant,[1] than did mine, and from none could more sincere and earnest prayers arise to the throne of Heaven, that hereafter slavery might only be known to Britain in the pages of her history. One shade alone obscured my pleasure, arising not from any difference in principle, but from the want of application of the general principle *to the whole empire*. The pious and able champions of *negro* liberty and *colonial* rights should, if I mistake not, have gone farther than they did; or, perhaps, to speak more correctly, before they had travelled so far as the

[1] An Anti-Slavery Meeting.

West Indies, should, at least for a few moments, have sojourned in our own immediate neighbourhood, and have directed the attention of the meeting to scenes of misery, acts of oppression, and victims of slavery, even on the threshold of our homes.

Let truth speak out, appalling as the statement may appear. The fact is true. Thousands of our fellow-creatures and fellow-subjects, both male and female, the miserable inhabitants of a *Yorkshire town* . . . are this very moment existing in a state of slavery, *more horrid* than the victims of that hellish system " *colonial slavery* ". . . . The very streets which receive the droppings of an " Anti-Slavery Society " are every morning wet by the tears of innocent victims at the accursed shrine of avarice . . . *the worsted mills in the town and neighbourhood of Bradford*! ! ! The nation is now most resolutely determined that negroes shall be free. Let them, however, not forget that Britons have common rights with Afric's sons. . . .

The factory system is necessary, but it is not necessarily an evil: it is conducive to the misery of many—it might be made advantageous to all. It is a system which drags in the train of the remorseless tyrant the man of benevolent mind; it compels the kind-hearted master either to relinquish business altogether, or in some measure to copy the cruelty of the oppressor. The system which impoverishes, enslaves and brutalises the labourer can never be advantageous to any country. The nation's strength and stability is built, if built for perpetuity, on the solid basis of a contented and happy population. The constitution of this country and the factory system cannot long exist together; and their principles are as opposite as light and darkness.

(ii) *Mammon-worship*

Thomas Carlyle was no party man, but it was in some kind of renewed and courageous Tory principle in society that he put his hope. Disraeli aped his style on at least one occasion (with painful results in a series of papers in *The Times* in 1838, under the title " Old England " and with the signature " Cœur-de-Lion "), and offered the old man a G.C.B. in 1874. There can be no doubt that books like *Past and Present* (1843) had a profound influence on the younger Tories of its day. Book III, Chapter 5, of *Past and Present* contains an appeal to Conservatism for courageous leadership. The following excerpts from *Past and Present* give some idea of Carlyle's diagnosis of the situation in the early eighteen-forties.

The saddest news is, that we should find our National Existence, as I sometimes hear it said, depend on selling manufactured cotton at a farthing an ell cheaper than any other People. A most narrow stand for a great Nation to base itself on! ... In brief, all this Mammon-Gospel of Supply-and-Demand, Competition, *Laissez-faire*, and Devil take the hindmost, begins to be one of the shabbiest Gospels ever preached; or altogether the shabbiest. . . . Farthing cheaper per yard! No great Nation can stand on the apex of such a pyramid; screwing itself higher and higher; balancing itself on its great-toe! ... The inventive genius of great England will not for ever sit patient with mere wheels and pinions, bobbins, straps and billy-rollers whirring in the head of it. The inventive genius of England is not a Beaver's, or a Spinner's or Spider's genius: it is a *Man's* genius, I hope, with a God over him! *Laissez-faire*, Supply-and-Demand—one begins to weary of all that. . . . Trade never so well freed, and Tariffs all settled or abolished, and Supply-and-Demand in full operation—let us all know that we have yet done nothing; that we have merely cleared the ground for doing.

I will venture to believe that in no time, since the beginnings of Society, was the lot of those same dumb millions of toilers so entirely unbearable as it is even in the days now passing over us. . . . That I have been called, by all the Newspapers, a " free man " will avail me little, if my pilgrimage have ended in death and wreck. . . . Liberty requires new definitions. . . . The liberty of not being oppressed by your fellow man is an indispensable yet one of the most insignificant fractional parts of Human Liberty. . . . The notion that a man's liberty consists of giving him the vote at election-hustings, and saying " Behold now I too have my twenty-thousandth part of a Talker in our National Palaver; will not all the gods be good to me? " is one of the pleasantest! . . . The liberty especially which has to purchase itself by social isolation, and each man standing separate from the other, having " no business with him " but a cash-account: this is such a liberty as the earth seldom saw—as the earth will not long put up with, recommend it how you may. . . . Brethren, we know but imperfectly yet, after ages of Constitutional Government, what Liberty and Slavery are.

(iii) *The Stolen Hour*

Lord John Manners, afterwards 7th Duke of Rutland, was perhaps the most lovable and idealistic member of the group of youthful aristocrats associated with Disraeli under the banner of " Young England " in the 1840's. The following is the famous passage of indignation from his speech on the Factory Act of 1844, when, on March 22 of that year, the House of Commons debated for many hours the critical question whether children should be allowed to work eleven hours instead of ten hours a day in the cotton-mills.

Let the question be divested of all extraneous matter, and what did it come to? Were the representatives of the people of England of opinion that 12 hours instead of 10 are a fitting duration for the labours of England's mothers and young children? That was the question, and the solution of it seemed to him easy; but then came the Honourable Members for Manchester, Stockport and the rest, and pleaded two propositions in bar: first, that the commerce and manufactures of this great Empire would be destroyed unless these mothers and children were allowed to work 12 hours a day, and, in the next place, that the wages of the work-people would be reduced. With something like indignation, with something like contempt, he begged to ask was this possible? It was saying to this country, it was affirming in the face of all Europe, that the whole secret of our vast manufacturing power lay in the one hour before sunrise, and the one hour after sunset, that we snatched from the poor people of England.

(iv) *The Thraldom of Capital*

The following section brings together a number of passages from the writings and speeches of Disraeli in the period when he was the leader of "Young England". It will be seen that Disraeli's underlying theme throughout is the irresponsibility of the middle-class industrial and commercial capitalist, the class which triumphed in 1832 and 1846. The parallels and contrasts which Carlyle had instituted between early Victorian England and the Middle Ages (*Past and Present*) are sharpened and deepened, so that the new baronage is a baronage without obligation, the new serfdom a serfdom without security, the new monastery a Poor-law Bastille. The first passage is from a speech on Miles's Amendment, in the House of Commons, February 20, 1846. The rest are from *Sybil* (1845).

ON THE REPEAL OF THE CORN-LAWS:

I must confess my deep mortification that in an age of political regeneration, when all social evils are ascribed to the operation of class interests, it should be suggested that we are to be rescued from the alleged power of one class only to sink under the avowed dominion of another . . . under the thraldom of capital —under those who, while they boast of their intelligence, are more proud of their wealth. . . .

ON THE REFORM ACT:

The Reform Act may have exercised on the country at large a beneficial influence. Has it? Has it elevated the tone of the public mind? Has it cultured the popular sensibilities to noble and ennobling ends? Has it proposed to the people of England a higher test of national respect and confidence than the debasing qualification universally prevalent in this country since the fatal introduction of the system of Dutch finance? Who will pretend it? If a spirit of rapacious covetousness, desecrating all the humanities of life, has been the besetting sin of England for the last century and a half, since the passing of the Reform Bill the altar of Mammon has blazed with triple worship. To acquire, to accumulate, to plunder each other by virtue of philosophic phrases, to propose a Utopia to consist only of Wealth and Toil, this has been the breathless business of enfranchised England for the last twelve years, until we are startled from our voracious strife by the wail of intolerable serfage.

THE NEW BARONAGE:

Now what is the fundamental principle of the feudal system, gentlemen? It is that the tenure of all property shall be the performance of its duties. . . . And when I see masses of property raised in this country which do not recognise that principle; when I find men making fortunes by a method which permits them (very often in a few years) to purchase the lands of the old territorial aristocracy of the country, I cannot help remembering that those millions are accumulated by a mode which does not recognise it as a duty " to endow the Church, to feed the poor, to guard the land, and to execute justice for nothing. . . ." When I know that evidence exists in our Parliament of a state of demoralisation in the once happy population of this land, which is not equalled in the most barbarous countries . . . I cannot help suspecting that this has arisen because property has been permitted to be created and held without the performance of its duties.

THE NEW SERFDOM:

There is more serfdom in England now than at any time since the Conquest. I speak of what passes under my daily eyes when I say that those who labour can as little choose their masters now as when they were born thralls. There are great bodies of the working classes of this country nearer the condition of brutes than they have been at any time since the Conquest.

THE NEW MONASTERIES:

The union workhouses. . . . They are building something for the people at last. After an experiment of three centuries, your gaols being full, and your treadmills losing something of their virtue, you have given us a substitute for the monasteries.

(v) *Summons to Toryism*

In the 1840's, when the values of the new world of industrial bondage and irresponsible economic power seemed to have infected even Conservatism with its Pittite cult of " The Wealth of Nations " and the harnessing of Big Business to the cause of " Conservation ", men like Carlyle, Richard Oastler, Lord John Manners, and the young Disraeli began to appeal to the great tradition of Toryism, popular, paternal, fraternal, even feudal, but above all courageously and passionately devoted to social justice. Out of this appeal, slowly and painfully, came that Tory Democracy which we now associate with Beaconsfield, Randolph Churchill, and the vanguard of twentieth-century Conservatism.

The remainder of this chapter will illustrate: first, the summons, then the response, which led Conservatism back to the finest traditions of its Tory heritage.

The following are a few types of the summons from a diversity of voices.

RICHARD OASTLER: Now Tories, what say you? Will you go back? You cannot. " Stand still "? Impossible. Will you join the Whigs against the people? If so you are a set of unprincipled knaves, and deserve to meet with the first reward of roguery. Will you go forward, then, hand in hand with " the people " and thus save the nation from anarchy and blood—thus secure the rights of the nobles by giving comfort, peace and contentment to the cottage? If you follow this plan, every patriot will join you, I care not whether he be Tory, Whig or Radical, every man who loves his country will be on your side. . . . The people have now learnt their strength, the avalanche is descending and will crush their opponents. It is not too late to guide it—it *is* too late to oppose. (1832)

LORD JOHN MANNERS: What I meant by wishing us [the Tories] to follow the example of the French Legitimists and assimilate our cause with that of the people, is easily explained. Let us show the people, i.e. the lower orders, by adding to their comforts and pleasures in the only legitimate way a legislature can do,—viz., by voting money to build public baths, to keep up—or rather to restore—public games, to form public walks, that we are their real friends. Let us give back the Church Holy-Days, open the Churches and Cathedrals to them, and let our men of power in their individual capacities assume a more personal and consequently a more kind intercourse with those below them. In a word, let society take a more feudal appearance than it presents now. That's my vision; it may be a wrong one; but if, as I believe, the Whig one of giving the people political power and prating to them of the rights of man, the glories of science, and the merits of political economy, is wrong, I can see no other way save the old worn-out one of *laissez-faire, laissez-aller*. . . . (1842)

THOMAS CARLYLE: O my Conservative friends, who still specially name and struggle to approve yourselves " Conservative," would to Heaven I could persuade you of this world-old fact, than which Fate is not surer, that Truth and Justice *alone* are capable of being " conserved " and preserved! The thing which is unjust, which is *not* according to God's law, will you, in a God's Universe, try to conserve that? It is so old, say you? Yes, and the hotter haste ought *you*, of all others to be in, to let it grow no older! If but the faintest whisper in your hearts intimate to you that it is not fair—hasten, for the sake of Conservatism itself, to probe it rigorously, to cast it forth at once and for ever if guilty. . . . And ye call yourselves Conservatives, Aristocracies: ought not honour and nobleness of mind,

if they had departed from all the earth elsewhere, to
find their last refuge with you? . . . The bough that is
dead shall be cut away, for the sake of the tree itself
. . . let the Conservatism that would preserve cut it
away. . . .

(vi) *From* laissez-faire *to Intervention:* (1) *Retrospect*

The remainder of this chapter will illustrate the growth and
acceptance by Conservatism of the conception of the "In-
strumental State": the use of the state's authority, within limits
prescribed by both expediency and principle, as an instrument
of social control and adjustment. Briefly, this meant a return to
an older tradition than that of Peel and Liberal-Toryism. Lord
Hugh Cecil has summarised this in Chapter VI of his book,
Conservatism (1912).

It is often assumed that Conservatism and Socialism
are directly opposed. But this is not completely true.
Modern Conservatism inherits the traditions of Toryism
which are favourable to the activity and authority of
the State. Indeed, Mr. Herbert Spencer attacked
Socialism as being in fact a revival of Toryism; he
called it " the new Toryism." And he was so far right,
that Toryism was on the side of authority and that it
was rather the Whigs, and still more the Liberals of
the second and third quarters of the nineteenth century,
who insisted on the dangers of State interference and
the importance of the liberty of the individual. Both
the central government and the local power of squire
and parson were, in earlier times, inclined to what we
should now call " paternal government ", and had no
sympathy with the unrestricted working of competition
or the principles of *laissez-faire*. That authority should
relieve suffering; that it should control and regulate
trade; that it should restrain luxury; that it should

suppress vice; that it should maintain religious truth:—
these were principles which appealed to our forefathers
as reasonable and especially to those among them who
were Tories. And in the nineteenth century, when
Liberalism enforced to the utmost the principle of
personal liberty, it was among Conservatives that the
authority and control of the State was defended and in
some instances enlarged and strengthened.

(vii) *From* laissez-faire *to Intervention:* (2) Laissez-faire
The following passage, in reported speech, from Lord
Liverpool's reply, as Prime Minister, to Lord Grey's motion in
the House of Lords, November 23, 1819, " that there never was
extensive discontent without great misgovernment " (the occasion
was the public outcry after the Peterloo Massacre), is representative of the *laissez-faire* Toryism which the party inherited from
Pitt, the disciple of Adam Smith. Lord Liverpool said:

Personally he sympathised deeply with the distress.
Every man must look with an anxious desire towards
any measure which was calculated to afford relief to
the lower classes of people in this country, and more
especially to the manufacturing population. But the
Legislature must proceed with great caution. Measures
of that kind could not be viewed as matters of indifference. If they did not effect good, it was possible
that they might do much harm, and he believed that
for one instance in which benefit was produced by
Legislative interference in matters of trade and commerce, ten cases might be pointed out in which injury
had been the consequence. This was a doctrine which
could not be too often or too strongly impressed on the
people of this country. They ought to be taught that
evils inseparable from the state of things should not
be charged on any government; and, on enquiry, it

would be found that by far the greater part of the miseries of which human nature complained were in all times and in all countries beyond the control of human legislation.

"How small of all the ills that men endure,
The part which Kings or States can cause or cure!"
He was arguing here in a statesman-like but peculiarly English spirit. The Legislature of no other country whatever has shown so vigilant and constant a solicitude for the welfare of the poorer classes; no other has so generally abstained from interference with the details and operations of trade; and it is almost equally demonstrable that the pre-eminent prosperity of our trading classes of every kind has been caused, or at least very greatly aided and promoted, by that judicious abstinence.

(viii) *From* laissez-faire *to Intervention:* (3) *Coleridge*

It was Conservative prophets like Coleridge, Carlyle, and Ruskin; Tory philanthropists with a conscience like Shaftesbury; humane and enlightened men of Tory principles within the manufacturing world itself, like Oastler, Sadler, and others; Tory "rebels" and feudal aristocrats like Disraeli, Lord John Manners, George Smythe, and the "Young England" group: it was these men, rather than the official and strictly political leaders of the Party, who brought the Conservative Party to accept the principle of state intervention on behalf of the distressed working classes. In 1818 Coleridge took up his pen to compose *Two Addresses on Sir Robert Peel's Bill* (1818). This Bill, promoted by the father of Sir Robert Peel, the Prime Minister, is generally known as the first Factory Act. Its terms were very mild. What is important here, however, is Coleridge's arguments in favour of intervention. The following passages are taken from the *Two Addresses* of 1818 (ed. by Sir Edmund Gosse, privately printed, 1913).

Now, in reply to the first objection [that legislative interference with free labour is improper] ... we might fairly enquire on what grounds is this impropriety presumed? Certainly not on past experience or the practice of the British Constitution; the Statute Books are (perhaps too much) crowded with proofs to the contrary. The first institution by law of Apprenticeships was an interference with free labour. . . . But if this objection to interference in free labour can derive no sanction from the *practice* of the Legislature, still less can it appeal to the *principles* and *spirit* of the British Constitution: and pardon us, if we add, God forbid that it should! . . . The *principle* of *all* constitutional law is to make the claims of each as much as possible compatible with the claims of all, as individuals, and with those of the commonwealth as a whole: and out of this adjustment, the claims of the individual first become *rights*. Every Canal Bill proves that there is no species of property which the legislature does not possess and exercise the right of controlling and limiting, as soon as the right of the individuals is shown to be disproportionately injurious to the community. . . .

But *free* labour!—in what sense, not utterly sophistical, can the labour of children, extorted from the want of their parents, " their poverty but not their will consenting ", be called *free*? . . . It is our duty to declare aloud, that if the labour were indeed free, the employer would purchase, and the labourer sell, what the former had no right to buy, and the latter no right to dispose of : namely, the labourer's health, life, and well-being. These belong not to himself *alone*, but to his friends, to his parents, to his King, to his Country, and to God. If the labour were indeed free, the contract would approach, on the one side, too near to suicide, on the other to manslaughter. The objection therefore would far better suit those who maintain the existence of rights, self-originated and independent of duties, than English subjects who pretend to no *rights* that do not refer to some *duty* as their origin and true foundation. . . .

Who, we would ask, are to be the judges whether the proposed measures will or will not be a serious diminution of the sufferings and evils complained of ? . . . Surely, either the sufferers or their parents and nearest relatives. But the latter are among the most earnest petitioners for this Bill: and . . . who does not know that in a journey too long for the traveller's strength, it is the last few miles that torment him by fatigue and injure him by exhaustion? . . . Substitute a child employed on tasks the most opposite to all its natural instincts, were it only from their improgressive and wearying uniformity—in a heated stifling impure atmosphere, fevered by noise and glare, both limbs and spirit outwearied—and that at the tenth hour he has still three, four, or five hours more to look forward to. Will he, will the poor little *sufferer,* be brought to believe that these hours are mere trifles—or the privilege of going home not worth his thanks? . . .

But we hasten to the . . . last objection, namely, that the reform of all these grievances may be safely trusted in these enlightened times to the good sense and humanity of the masters themselves. This is doubtless highly flattering to the present age, and still more so to that which is to follow. It is, however, sufficient for us to have proved that it remains a mere assertion. . . . The age had been complimented with the epithets of enlightened, humane, etc., years before the abolition of the Slave Trade. And was that Trade abolished by the increasing humanity, the enlightened self-interest, of the slave-owners? . . .

(ix) *From* laissez-faire *to Intervention:* (4) *Lord Shaftesbury*

Antony Ashley Cooper, 7th Earl of Shaftesbury, lived from 1801 to 1885, and almost the whole of his long life was devoted to campaigning for legislative intervention on behalf of factory operatives, colliery workers, chimney-sweeping boys and the reclamation of the children of the poor. His inspiration was a farouche and intolerant form of Evangelical Christianity, and his motive was to win the working classes of England not for the Tory Party but for Heaven. Nevertheless, Shaftesbury, like John Wesley, was an out-and-out Tory, and it is important to realise that Toryism was not merely associated with the High Anglican tradition of social responsibility represented by men like the young Gladstone and Lord John Manners, but also with the Evangelicalism that so often is associated with Whiggery and Liberalism. Shaftesbury represents this strain of Tory-Evangelicalism, and the following passage from an article on " Infant Labour " which he contributed to the *Quarterly Review* in December 1840 gives some idea of the motivation and objects of this type of Toryism. It will be seen to have been a strong ally of legislative intervention, but poles apart from Tory Democracy. Its business was to plead for, but never to appeal to, the people. Shaftesbury himself thought Peel's Conservatism a betrayal of the Tory cause, and deplored Disraeli's Reform Act of 1867 as bitterly as Carlyle, or any authoritarian of the age. The type is represented in the present chapter for its alliance with legislative interventionism only.

The two great demons in morals and politics, Socialism and Chartism, are stalking through the land; yet they are but symptoms of an universal disease, spread throughout vast masses of the people, who, so far from concurring in the *status quo*, suppose that anything must be better than their present condition. . . . Our system begets the vast and inflammable mass that lies waiting, day by day, for the spark to explode it into mischief. We cover the land with spectacles of misery; wealth is felt only by its oppressions. . . . No wonder that thousands of hearts should be against a system which establishes the relations, without calling forth the mutual sympathies of master and servant, landlord and tenant, employer and employed. We need not to express our firm belief that there are beneficent and blessed exceptions; but generally speaking, in those districts and those departments of industry the rich and poor are antagonist parties, each watching an opportunity to gain an advantage over the other. . . . When called upon to suggest our remedy of the evil, we reply by an exhibition of the cause of it; the very statement involves an argument, and contains its own answer within itself. Let your laws, we say to the Parliament, assume the proper functions of law, protect those for whom neither wealth, nor station, nor age has raised a bulwark against tyranny; but, above all, open your treasury, erect churches, send forth the ministers of religion, reverse the conduct of the enemy of mankind, and sow wheat among the tares—all hopes are groundless, all legislation weak, all conservatism nonsense, without this alpha and omega of policy; it will give content instead of bitterness, engraft obedience on rebellion, raise purity from corruption, and " life from the dead ".

CHAPTER 7

TORY DEMOCRACY: DISRAELI AND RANDOLPH CHURCHILL

Tory Democracy, with its devotion to the national institutions and its readiness to invoke legislative authority in the interests of social justice, found its supreme vindication in the achievements of Disraeli's Administration of 1874–1880. It was a Labour Member of Parliament, Alexander Macdonald, who said that "the Conservative party have done more for the working classes in five years than the Liberals have done in fifty."

Disraeli died in 1881, and when Lord Salisbury came into power in 1885 it seemed for a time that the mantle of Elisha had fallen upon the young Randolph Churchill. A son of one of the patrician families of England, Churchill was a democrat and a social reformer, while his chief, Lord Salisbury, was a die-hard. It seemed in the 'eighties that Churchill's "Fourth Party"—of which Henry Drummond Wolff, John Gorst, and (for a time) Arthur Balfour were members—was to serve the educative and enlivening purpose served by Disraeli and "Young England" in the days of Peel and Derby. But Randolph Churchill was not only brilliant; he was perverse, impatient, and over-confident of his own indispensability. He died at the age of forty-six, still scarcely more than the *enfant terrible* of Conservatism. He was, as his son, Mr. Winston Churchill, has said in his biography of his father, "a great elemental force in British politics"—a power over the imagination and sympathies of the young men who were to make the party of the twentieth century. His was the kind of career, and the kind of influence, that can scarcely be assessed in the common terms of concrete achievement.

(i) *"Popular Principles" and "Liberal Opinions"*

Perhaps the main element in Tory Democracy, as defined by Disraeli and Churchill, is its insistence on the primacy of national over sectional interests. Negatively, Tory Democracy expressed itself in an attack on the sectionalism of Liberalism. The idea that "popular" principles are shared by high and low, while "liberal" opinions are the prejudices of a selfish middle class, is a pre-supposition of Tory Democracy. What Disraeli was saying of the Whigs, and the spirit of Whiggism, in 1834, he was saying of Liberalism in 1847. The passage given below is taken from his address to the electors of the County of Bucks in that year.

In the great struggle between popular principles and liberal opinions, which is the characteristic of our age, I hope ever to be found on the side of the people, and of the Institutions of England. . . . Liberal opinions are the opinions of those who would be free from certain constraints and regulations, from a certain dependence and duty which are deemed necessary for the general and popular welfare. Liberal opinions are very convenient opinions for the rich and the powerful. They ensure enjoyment and are opposed to self-sacrifice. The holder of Liberal opinions, for example, maintains that the possession of land is to be considered in a commercial light and no other. He looks to the income which it will afford him. It is not a Liberal principle that the holder of land should incur the duty of executing justice and maintaining truth among the multitude for nothing. That, gentlemen, is a popular principle, a principle of government for the benefit of the people, not a Liberal opinion. A poor law is founded upon a popular principle: Liberal opinions are entirely averse to its enactments. . . . Instead of royalty, a gentleman of Liberal opinions would prefer that the supreme executive should be entrusted to a person of his own class, with the title of President, and perhaps to have the chance of becoming President himself; instead of a national Church he prefers to choose and pay for his own minister of religion, if he has a wish for one; and although he is not averse to the theory of representative government, provided the representation is absorbed by his own order, he encourages the real transaction of affairs to be conducted by paid commissioners and select committees.

(ii) *Disraeli re-states the basis of Toryism*

Disraeli's education of his party might be summed up as a process of recovery: recovery of the original and historic elements of Toryism. It was, at the same time, a process of interpretation: the interpretation of original Tory principles within the setting of the modern world. In the following passages we find him engaged in this re-statement in the years 1862 and 1863. The first paragraph is from a speech in Parliament in 1862, and the second from a speech at a dinner-party in the following year. Both are to be found in Monypenny and Buckle's *Life of Disraeli*, Vol. IV, Chapter 10.

Ever since that period of disaster and dismay, when my friends and myself were asked for the first time to sit upon these benches,[1] it has ever been our habit, in counselling the Tory party, to recur gradually but most sincerely to the original elements of that great political connection. To build up a community, not upon Liberal opinions, which anyone may fashion to his fancy, but upon popular principles,[2] which assert equal rights, civil and religious; to uphold the institutions of the country because they are the embodiments of the wants and wishes of the nation, and protect us alike from individual tyranny and popular outrage; equally to resist democracy and oligarchy, and favour that

[1] 1847.

[2] See section ii, above.

principle of free aristocracy which is the only basis and security for constitutional government; to be vigilant to guard and prompt to vindicate the honour of the country, but to hold aloof from that turbulent diplomacy which only distracts the mind of a people from internal improvement; to lighten taxation; frugally but wisely to administer the public treasure; to favour popular education, because it is the best guarantee for public order; to defend local government, and to be as jealous of the rights of the working man as of the prerogative of the Crown and the privileges of the senate—these were once the principles which regulated Tory statesmen, and I for one have no wish that the Tory party should ever be in power unless they practise them.

The Tory party is only in its proper position when it represents popular principles. Then it is truly irresistible. Then it can uphold the throne and the altar, the majesty of the empire, the liberty of the nation, and the rights of the multitude. There is nothing mean, petty, or exclusive, about the real character of Toryism. It necessarily depends upon enlarged sympathies and noble aspirations, because it is essentially national.

(iii) *Tory Democracy as defined by Randolph Churchill*
The following passage is from a speech by Lord Randolph Churchill at Manchester, November 6, 1885. Churchill was at this time Secretary for India in Lord Salisbury's first ministry. The passage shows very clearly its author's conscious assumption of the mantle of Disraeli within some four years of the great statesman's death.

What is the Tory democracy that the Whigs should deride it and hold it to the execration of the people? It has been called a contradiction in terms; it has been described as a nonsensical appellation. I believe it to be the most simple and the most easily understood political denomination ever assumed. The Tory democracy is a democracy which has embraced the principles of the Tory party. It is a democracy which believes that an hereditary monarchy and hereditary House of Lords are the strongest fortifications which the wisdom of man, illuminated by the experience of centuries, can possibly devise for the protection, not of Whig privilege, but of democratic freedom. The Tory democracy is a democracy which adheres to and will defend the Established Church, because it believes that Establishment is a guarantee of State morality, and that the connection between Church and State imparts to the ordinary functions of executive and law something of a divine sanction. The Tory democracy is a democracy which, under the shadow and under the protection of those great and ancient institutions, will resolutely follow the path of administrative reform.

(iv) " *Trust the People* "

The famous speech bearing this name was delivered by Lord Randolph Churchill at Birmingham on April 16, 1884. It was the year of Gladstone's Parliamentary Reform Act. Churchill's speech is worth quotation at some length, containing as it does his best-known reiteration of the classic Disraelian doctrine of Conservatism's attachment to the national institutions as the great bulwarks of freedom, and his most effective public statement of the party's claims to be the party of the people.

What is the great and wide difference which distinguishes the two great political parties who endeavour to attract the support of the English people? It has been well and wisely said—but I do not think it can be too often repeated—that the Tory party clings with veneration and affection to the institutions of our country. The Radicals regard them with aversion and distrust and will always give multitudinous and specious reasons for their destruction. But how can we, the Tory party, give no good convincing reasons to the people for the faith which is in us? We do not defend the Constitution from mere sentiment for the past, or from any infatuated superstition about Divine right or hereditary excellence. We defend the Constitution solely on the ground of its utility to the people. It is on the ground of utility alone that we go forth to meet our foes, and if we fail to make good our ground with utilitarian arguments and for utilitarian ends, then let the present combination of Throne, Lords and Commons be for ever swept away.

An hereditary throne is the surest device that has ever been imagined or invented for the perpetuation of civil order and for that first necessity of civilised society—continuity of government . . . it would be impossible to devise a form of governmental summit as effectual, and yet cheaper and more simple. . . .

I maintain that the House of Lords should be preserved solely on the ground of its utility to the people. I do not put forward as an argument for its preservation its long history, in order to show you that it possesses great merit as an institution. I do not argue, as some do, that it has acquired stability from the circumstance that by its composition it is rooted in the soil. I content myself with the fact of its existence at the present moment, and I find in it not only a powerful check on popular impulses arising from imperfect information, not only an aggregate of political wisdom and experience such as no other country can produce, but, above all, because I find it literally the only effec-tual barrier against that most fatal foe to freedom, the one-man power. . . . From a national and imperial point of view, you need never be alarmed at the dangers of one-man power so long as the House of Lords endures. Be he minister, be he capitalist, be he demagogue . . . against that bulwark of popular liberty and civil order, he will dash himself in vain. The House of Lords may, perhaps, move slowly; they may, perhaps, be over-cautious about accepting the merits of the legislation of the House of Commons; they may, perhaps, at times regard with some exaggeration of sentiment the extreme rights of property. That is the price you have to pay—and a small price it is for so valuable a possession—which guards you against so great a danger. They are essentially of the people. Year by year they are recruited from the people. Every privilege, every franchise, every liberty which is gained by the people, is treasured up and guarded by those who, animated by tradition and custom, by long descent and lofty name, fear neither monarchs, nor ministers, nor men, but only the people, whose trustees they are. . . .

I cannot pass from this subject of the House of Lords without alluding to that other bugbear of the Radical party, the Church of England, and its connection with the State. . . . Again I adhere to my utilitarian line of defence, and I would urge upon you not to lend yourselves too hastily to any project for the demolition of the Established Church. But I would also, in dealing with this question, mingle a little of the wine of sentiment with the cold clear spring water of utilitarianism.

. . . I see in the Church of England an immense and omnipresent ramification of machinery working without cost to the people—and daily and hourly lifting the masses of the people, rich and poor alike, from the dead and dreary level of the lowest and most material cares of life, up to the comfortable contemplation of higher and serener forms of existence and of destiny. I see in the Church of England a centre and a source and a guide of charitable effort, mitigating by its mendicant importunity the violence of human misery. . . . And I urge upon you not to throw that source of charity upon the haphazard almsgiving of a busy and a selfish world. I view the Church of England eagerly co-operating in the work of national education, not only benefiting your children but saving your pockets; and I remember that it has been the work of the Church to pour forth floods of knowledge, purely secular and scientific, even from the days when knowledge was not; and I warn you against hindering the diffusion of knowledge, inspired by religion, amongst those who will have devolved upon them the responsibility for the government of this wide Empire.

But I own that my chief reason for supporting the Church of England I find in the fact that, when compared with other creeds and other sects, it is essentially the Church of religious liberty. Whether in one direction or another, it is continually possessed by the ambition, not of excluding, but of including, all shades of religious thought, all sorts and conditions of men. . . . I cannot, and will not, allow myself to believe that the English people, who are not only naturally religious, but also eminently practical . . . will ever consent to deprive themselves of so abundant a fountain of aid and consolation, or acquiesce in the demolition of an institution which elevates the life of the nation and consecrates the acts of State. . . .

Last, but not least—no; rather first—in the scheme of Tory politics come the Commons of England. . . .

The social progress of the Commons by means of
legislative reform under the lines and carried on under
the protection of the institutions whose utility I have
endeavoured to describe to you—that must be the policy
of the Tory party. . . . No class interests should be
allowed to stand in the way of this mighty movement,
and with this movement, the Tory party not only sym-
pathise, but identify themselves. Social reform, producing direct and immediate benefit to the Commons—that
must be our cry, as opposed to the Radicals, who fool-
ishly scream for organic change, and waste their
energies and their time in attacking institutions whose
destruction would not only endanger popular freedom,
but would leave the social condition of the people
precisely where it was . . .

" Trust the people "—I have long tried to make that
my motto; but I know, and will not conceal, that there
are still a few in our party who have that lesson yet
to learn and have yet to understand that the Tory party
of to-day is no longer identified with that small and
narrow class which is connected with the ownership
of land; but that its great strength can be found, and
must be developed, in our large towns as well as in our
country districts. Yes, trust the people. You, who are
ambitious, and rightly ambitious, of being the guardians
of the British Constitution, trust the people, and they
will trust you—and they will follow you and join you
in the defence of that Constitution against any and
every foe. I have no fear of democracy. . . . Modern
checks and securities are not worth a brass farthing.
Give me a fair arrangement of the constituencies, and
one part of England will correct and balance the other.

I do not think that electoral reform is a matter of
national emergency. . . . But you may be sure that the

English Constitution will endure and thrive, whether you add two millions of electors or two hundred to the electoral roll, so long as the Tory party is true to its past, mindful of its history, faithful to the policy that was bequeathed to it by Lord Beaconsfield. The future of the Constitution, the destinies of the Empire, are in the hands of the Tory party; and if only the leaders of the party in Parliament will have the courage of their convictions, grasp their responsibilities, and adapt their policy to those responsibilities, and if they are supported and stimulated by you who are here to-night, and by others like you in our large towns, that future and those destinies are great and assured. To rally the people round the Throne, to unite the Throne with the people, a loyal Throne and a patriotic people, that is our policy and that is our faith.

(v) *Conservatism and the Electorate*

We have seen how, after the passing of the first Reform Bill, Conservatism, with Peel's encouragement, went out to organise the new electorate by means of " Registration Societies ". With the further extension of the electorate in 1867 and 1884–85, something more elaborate was needed. Randolph Churchill expended much energy on this problem. It was plain that a party which proposed to " trust the people " and to seek to capture *urban* England, would have to enter the lists armed with the most modern weapons. There had been, since 1880, a " Central Committee " of the Conservative Party: a close body, largely identified with wealthy, sectional interests, wedded to aristocratic privilege and obsolete social ideas, and controlling the party funds very much as it pleased. Randolph Churchill, on the other hand, put his faith in the National Union of Conservative Associations, a body based on popular representation, with branches all over the country, and particularly active in the large towns. It was through this body, of whose council he was a co-opted member, that Churchill worked to wrest control of the party from the exclusive " Central Committee " and to bring the principles and policies of a democratic Conservatism home to the people, and more especially to the people of the industrial towns.

The first passage below is from Churchill's speech at the Conservative Conference in October 1883, when he attacked the Central Committee for keeping the National Union in what he called "a state of tutelage, if not of slavery", and laid down his conception of a democratic party organisation. The second passage is from a letter Churchill wrote on resigning his candidature for Birmingham in April 1884, in consequence of his views having been tacitly rejected by a majority on the council.

The Conservative Party will never exercise power until it has gained the confidence of the working classes; and the working classes are quite determined to govern themselves, and will not be either driven or hoodwinked by any class or class interests. . . . If you want to gain the confidence of the working classes, let them have a share, and a large share, a real share, not a sham share, in your party Councils and in your party government.

A popular organisation and a popular policy follow naturally the one upon the other, and without the former you will not have the latter. The efforts of the Council from the outset met with the strongest opposition from those who have great influence with the leaders of the party, who at present control such organisation as exists and dispense in irresponsible secrecy the considerable funds subscribed for party purposes. . . . The jealous guardians of aristocratic privilege have proved for the time too powerful for those who would base the strength of the Tory party upon the genuine and spontaneous attachment of the masses of our people. The interests of the many are still to be sacrificed to the love of power and interested ambition of a favoured few.

(vi) *Labour and the Future*

Towards the ends of his short life, some three years before his death, Randolph Churchill gave expression, in a letter to a Liberal-Unionist, to his views on the prospective arrival of Labour at the head of the state. He professes to feel no alarm at the prospect, but appeals once again for the enlistment of the labouring masses in support of the Constitutional party. The letter is given in Chapter XXII of Mr Winston Churchill's *Life* of his father.

The Labour interest is now seeking to do itself what the landed interest and the manufacturing capitalist interest did for themselves when each in turn commanded the disposition of State policy. Our land laws were framed by the landed interest for the advantage of the landed interest, and foreign policy was directed by that interest to the same end. Political power passed very considerably from the landed interest to the manufacturing capitalist interest, and our whole fiscal system was shaped by this latter power to its own advantage, foreign policy being also made to coincide. We are now come, or are coming fast, to a time when Labour laws will be made by the Labour interest for the advantage of Labour. The regulation of all the conditions of Labour by the State, controlled and guided by the Labour vote, appears to be the ideal aimed at. . . . Personally, I can discern no cause for alarm in this prospect. . . . Labour in this modern movement has against it the prejudices of property, the resources of capital, and all the numerous forces—social, professional and journalist—which those prejudices and resources can influence. It is our business as Tory politicians to uphold the Constitution. If under the Constitution as it now exists, and as we wish to see it preserved, the Labour interest finds that it can obtain its objects and secure its own advantage, then that interest will be reconciled to the Constitution, will find faith in it and will maintain it. But if it should unfortunately occur that the Constitutional party . . . are deaf to hear and slow to meet the demands of Labour, are stubborn in opposition to those demands and are persistent in the habit of ranging themselves in unreasoning and short-sighted support of all the present rights of property and capital, the result may be that the Labour interest may identify what it will take to be the defects in the Constitutional party with the Constitution itself, and in a moment of indiscriminate impulse may use its power to sweep both away.

CHAPTER 8

THE IMPERIAL TRADITION:
DISRAELI AND CHAMBERLAIN

Between the fall of Randolph Churchill and the Conservative revival of the present century, the only noteworthy development in the tradition is to be found in the field of Imperialism. Here, the Radical energies of Joseph Chamberlain brought to the party a vision of a federated Empire, a Commonwealth of Nations, knit together by a scheme of preferential tariffs and by some dimly envisaged organ of common consultation. Chamberlain's campaign for Tariff Reform was inspired by the need, as he saw it, for Imperial unity based upon economic· reciprocation. It developed, however, into a campaign for total abrogation of the Free Trade tradition which had governed English commercial policy since the days of Cobden, and it was sought to justify this momentous change as beneficial to both agricultural and industrial employment. It failed to convince the electorate on these grounds, and contributed to the downfall of Conservatism at the elections of 1906. Whether Joseph Chamberlain was, as some believe, a disaster for Conservatism, or, as more believe, one of its greatest prophets in modern times, Tariff Reform as he conceived it has remained a part of the tradition of the party in the twentieth century and requires to be illustrated in any documentation of the tradition down to 1914.

(i) *The modern conception of the Empire is born*
     From 1783 down to about 1870 the Empire grew without plan and without welcome from the home government—and virtually without interest on the part of the British public. After 1870, which year saw the founding of the German Empire, the age of Imperialism begins—an age of scramble, monopoly, and exclusion. It was Disraeli who sounded the new note in Britain, in a speech at the Crystal Palace on June 24, 1872. His speech

contained a good deal of partisan exaggeration in its strictures on the failure of the Liberals to maintain and cherish the Empire in the past: for the Tory failure had been no less complete. It is nevertheless true that from this speech, as Monypenny and Buckle claim, " the modern conception of the British Empire largely takes its rise ".

If you look to the history of this country since the advent of Liberalism—forty years ago—you will find that there has been no effort so continuous, so subtle, supported by so much ability and acumen, as the attempts of Liberalism to effect the disintegration of the Empire of England. And, gentlemen, of all its efforts, this is the one which has been the nearest to success. Statesmen of the highest character, writers of the most distinguished ability, the most organised and efficient means, have been employed in this endeavour. It has been proved to all of us that we have lost money by our colonies. It has been shown with precise, with mathematical demonstration, that there never was a jewel in the Crown of England that was so truly costly as the possession of India. How often has it been suggested that we should at once emancipate ourselves from this incubus. Well, that result was nearly accomplished. When those subtle views were adopted by the country under the plausible plea of granting self-government to the Colonies, I confess that I myself thought that the tie was broken. Not that I, for one, object to self-government; I cannot conceive how our distant Colonies can have their affairs administered except by self-government.

But self-government, in my opinion, when it was conceded, ought to have been conceded as part of a great policy of Imperial consolidation. It ought to have been accompanied by an Imperial Tariff, by securities for the people of England for the enjoyment of the unappropriated lands which belonged to the Sovereign as their trustee, and by a military code which should have precisely defined the means and the responsibilities by which the Colonies should be defended, and by which, if necessary, this country should call for aid from the Colonies themselves. It ought, further, to have been accompanied by the institution of some representative council in the metropolis, which would have brought the Colonies into constant and continuous relations with the Home Government. All this, however, was omitted because those who advised that policy—and I believe their convictions were sincere — looked upon the Colonies of England, looked even upon our connection with India, as a burden upon this country; viewing everything in a financial aspect, and totally passing by those moral and political considerations which make nations great, and by the influence of which alone men are distinguished from animals.

Well, what has been the result of this attempt during the reign of Liberalism for the disintegration of the Empire? It has entirely failed. But how has it failed? Through the sympathy of the Colonies for the Mother Country. They have decided that the Empire shall not be destroyed; and in my opinion no Minister in this country will do his duty who neglects any opportunity of reconstructing as much as possible of our Colonial Empire, and of responding to those distant sympathies which may become the source of incalculable strength and happiness to this land. . . .

The issue is no mean one. It is whether you will be content to be a comfortable England, modelled and moulded upon Continental principles and meeting in due course an inevitable fate, or whether you will be a great country, an imperial country, a country where your sons, when they rise, rise to paramount positions, and obtain not merely the esteem of their countrymen, but command the respect of the world.

(ii) *The Imperial Mission*

Disraeli had struck the two notes which dominate Conservative Imperialism henceforth: the note of " mission " or " vocation " as regards the Dependencies of the Crown, and the note of organisation as regards the self-governing Dominions. The two passages which follow illustrate the first: the theme of " mission ", as regards the dependencies. The one is by Lord Hugh Cecil, from his *Conservatism* (1912), and the other from a speech by Joseph Chamberlain at the Royal Colonial Institute on March 31, 1897. Chamberlain had already declared, two years earlier, that he regarded " many of our colonies as being in the condition of undeveloped estates . . . estates which never can be developed without imperial assistance." As Colonial Secretary, he proposed to implement this idea by devoting the income from Disraeli's Suez Canal shares (some £670,000 a year by this time) to a fund for Colonial development loans and investment. The scheme was not adopted until the establishment of the Colonial Development Fund in 1940.

We must say that national existence means the capacity to fulfil the national vocation. . . . Our vocation in the world has been to undertake the government of vast uncivilised populations and to raise them gradually to a higher level of life. Those populations form part of the Empire, but naturally can scarcely be reckoned as adding to its strength, at any rate in the earlier stages of development under our rule. After a time, as in India, they pass from being a sphere of national work to being a part of the national strength; and if there are deductions to be made, those may fairly be reckoned as signs of the imperfection that attaches to all human effort. In what we call the Dependencies of the Crown, therefore, there is nothing abnormal, nothing inconsistent with the obvious characteristics of our vocation.

But the British Empire is not confined to the self-governing colonies and the United Kingdom. It includes a much greater area, a much more numerous population in tropical climes, where no considerable European settlement is possible, and where the native population must always vastly outnumber the white inhabitants; and in these cases also the same change has come over the Imperial idea. Here also the sense of possession has given place to a different sentiment — the sense of obligation. We feel now that our rule over these territories can only be justified if we can show that it adds to the happiness and prosperity of the people; and I maintain that our rule does, and has brought security and peace and comparative prosperity to countries that never knew these blessings before.

In carrying out this work of civilisation we are fulfilling what I believe to be our national mission, and we are finding scope for the exercise of those faculties and qualities which have made of us a great governing race. I do not say that our success has been perfect in every case, I do not say that all our methods have been beyond reproach; but I do say that in almost every instance in which the rule of the Queen has been established and the great *Pax Britannica* has been enforced, there has come with it greater security to life and property, and a material improvement in the condition of the bulk of the population.

(iii) *Problems of Imperial Organisation*

Disraeli's second theme, that of Imperial organisation, was to become the principal concern of the later career of Joseph

Chamberlain. As an introduction to this, the following passage from Lord Cecil's *Conservatism* (1912) will serve to outline the nature of the issues involved.

The greatest problem of imperial affairs [is] the problem of how to make the Empire a single organism without destroying or imperilling the full liberty which each part of it rightly and uncompromisingly claims. We want the peoples of the Dominions to be in the fullest sense part of the national power. We want them to hearken with a single ear to the dictates of the national vocation. We want the whole body to go forth on its appointed task with a single mind and will. But we want also that all citizen of our race, in whatever part of the King's Dominions they may live, shall be equally sharers in the great inheritance of free self-government. To the solution of this problem Conservatism is already addressing itself. Nor is there any partisan dispute about the ultimate purpose in view. The policy of preferential trade has been propounded as a step in the desired direction; and if this policy has been resisted by Liberals and a few Conservatives, it is not because its unifying object is not desired, but because there are doubts as to the reality of its unifying effect. It is disputed whether giving British subjects in different parts of the Empire trade advantages at the cost of other British subjects in the imperial markets, will really make for unifying and organising the whole body. But the policy of drawing the whole Empire together is and will remain a chief object of Conservatism to-day; and if it should turn out that preference is an impossible or inefficacious method of achieving the object, it will only serve to turn the minds of Conservatives to new expedients for attaining what they desire. . . .

We do not desire to press the cause of union in a way inconsistent with the facts of distance, and consequently with well-informed and skilful government. We do not, in short, wish to interfere with any powers the colonial Dominions now possess. But we wish to bring them into activity as part of the operative power of the Empire as a whole, in order that a single national unit may fulfil to the world its appointed vocation.

(iv) *The Prospects of Federation*, 1897

Joseph Chamberlain discusses the prospects of Empire Federation in a speech to the Royal Colonial Institute, March 31, 1897, and at the Colonial Conference, 24 June of the same year.

(a)

We want to promote a closer and firmer union between all members of the great British race, and in this respect we have in recent years made great progress —so great that I think sometimes some of our friends are apt to be a little hasty, and to expect even a miracle to be accomplished. I would like to ask them to remember that time and patience are essential elements in the development of all great ideas. Let us, gentlemen, keep our ideal always before us. For my own part I believe in the practical possibility of a federation of the British race, but I know that it will come, if it does come, not by pressure, not by anything in the nature of dictation from this country, but it will come as the realisation of a universal desire, as the expression of the dearest wish of our colonial fellow-subjects themselves.

(b)

Strong as is the bond of sentiment, and impossible as it would be to establish any kind of relations unless that bond of sentiment existed, I believe we all feel that it would be desirable to take advantage of it, and to still further tighten the ties which bind us together. In this country, at all events, I may truly say that the idea of federation is in the air, whether with you it has gone as far, it is for you to say, and it is also for you to consider whether we can give any practical application to the principle. It may well be that the time is hardly ripe for anything definite in this regard. It is quite true that our own constitutions and your constitutions have all been the subject of very slow growth and that they are all the stronger because they have been gradually consolidated, and so perhaps with Imperial Federation: if it is ever to be accomplished, it will be only after the lapse of a considerable time and only by gradual steps. . . .

I feel that there is a real necessity for some better machinery of consultation between the self-governing colonies and the mother-country, and it has sometimes struck me—I offer it now merely as a personal suggestion—that it might be feasible to create a great council of the Empire to which the colonies would send representative plenipotentiaries, not mere delegates who were unable to speak in their name, without further reference to their respective governments, but persons who, by their position in the colonies, by their representative character, and by their close touch with colonial feeling, would be able, upon all subjects submitted to them, to give really effective and valuable advice. If such a council were to be created it would at once assume an immense importance, and it is perfectly evident that it might develop into something still greater. It might slowly grow to that Federal Council to which we must always look forward as our ultimate ideal.

(v) *Imperial Union and Tariff Reform*

On May 15, 1903, Chamberlain addressed his constituents at Birmingham on his return from his tour of South Africa, and "initiated the acute stage of the fiscal controversy." In November of that year, the Tariff Reform League issued a reprint of some of his speeches on that subject in the course of the year, and the following summary of his arguments was supplied by Chamberlain himself by way of an introduction.

The changes that have taken place since the adoption of Free Trade nearly sixty years ago in the conditions of international exchange, in the comparative position of foreign nations, and, above all, in our relations with our own colonies, seem to point conclusively to the necessity of a reconsideration of our fiscal system.

The original object of Mr. Cobden and his colleagues was to secure a free exchange of products between the nations of the world at their natural price, but for many years the example of the open door set by the United Kingdom has not been followed by other countries, and hostile tariffs have everywhere interfered with the natural course of trade.

These tariffs, avowedly designed to exclude British manufactures, have been supported by the operation of bounties, subsidies and trusts; while foreign producers have been enabled, partly by the same means, and partly by the lower standard of living to which their working classes are accustomed, to undersell the British manufacturer in neutral markets, and even seriously attack his home trade.

The doctrinaire Free Traders have no remedy to propose for this state of things, which, indeed, they either deny, or else ascribe to the want of enterprise and intelligence on the part of our manufacturers, to the ignorance and incapacity of our people, or to the tyrannical action of the Trade Unions.

The Tariff Reformers, on the other hand, believe that by recovering their freedom of action, and by re-arming ourselves with the weapon of a moderate tariff, we may still defend our home market against unfair competition, and may, at the same time, secure a modification of foreign tariffs which would open the way to a fairer exchange of our respective products than we have hitherto been able to obtain.

But they attach even greater importance to the possibility of securing by preferential and reciprocal arrangements with our colonies a great development of trade within the Empire and a nearer approach to a commercial union which, in some shape or another, must precede or accompany closer political relations, and without which, as all history shows, no permanent co-operation is possible.

They believe that these objects can be promoted, without loss to any class or any individual, by a slight transfer of existing taxes which will not increase national burdens, but will raise the revenue required for defence and administration in such a way as to develop our inter-imperial trade to the mutual benefit both of the colonies and the mother country, while adding greatly to the amount of employment for our ever-growing population.

The questions thus raised, although they interest every class, are more vitally important to working men than to any other, since they alone depend upon their daily employment for their daily subsistence.

(vi) *Imperial Preference and Imperial Unity*

The following passage from Chamberlain's speech of May 15, 1903, to his Birmingham constituents, develops further the Imperial argument which forms only one element in the above summary: as does the subjoined passage from a speech at Glasgow in October 1903.

(a)

But the question of trade and commerce is one of the greatest importance. Unless that is satisfactorily settled, I, for one, do not believe in a continued union of the Empire. . . . I say it is the business of British statesmen to do everything they can, even at some present sacrifice, to keep the trade of the colonies with Great Britain; to increase that trade, to promote it, even if in doing so we lessen somewhat the trade with our foreign competitors. . . . Are we, in fact, by our legislation, by our action, making for union, or are we drifting to separation? That is a critical issue. In my opinion, the germs of a Federal Union that will make the British Empire powerful and influential for good beyond the dreams of any one now living are in the soil; but it is a tender and delicate plant, and requires careful handling. . . . And, for my own part, I believe in a British Empire, in an Empire which, although it should be one of its first duties to cultivate friendship with all the nations of the world, should yet, even if alone, be self-sustaining and self-sufficient, able to maintain itself against the competition of all its rivals.

(b)

Can we invent a tie which must be a practical one, which will prevent separation? . . . I make the same answer as Mr. Rhodes, who suggested reciprocal preference, and I say that it is only by commercial union, reciprocal preference, that you can lay the foundations of the confederation of the Empire to which we all look forward as a brilliant possibility. Now I have told you what you are to gain by preference. You will gain the retention and the increase of your customers. You will gain work for the enormous number of those who are now unemployed; you will pave the way for a firmer and more enduring union of the Empire. What will it cost you? What do the colonies ask? They ask a preference on their particular products. . . . Therefore, if you wish to have preference, if you desire to gain this increase, if you wish to prevent separation, you must put a tax on food. The murder is out . . . [But in the remarks of my opponents you] never see attached to this statement that you must tax food the other words that I have used in reference to this subject, that nothing that I propose would add one farthing to the cost of living to the working man, or to any family in this country. . . . I do not believe that these small taxes upon food would be paid to any large extent by the consumers in this country. I believe, on the contrary, they would be paid by the foreigner.

(vii) *Tariff Reform and the Working Classes*

Chamberlain was at great pains to show that Tariff Reform was not "a rich man's question" and to bring home to the working classes his contention that it was calculated to improve employment and wages. He brought this out particularly forcibly in two speeches in 1904–5, the first at Limehouse on December 15, 1904, and the second at Gainsborough on February 1, 1905.

(a)

[After a résumé of factory legislation and social interventionism on behalf of the working classes]: This attempt of ours to raise the general standard of living, to regulate the conditions of trade in the interest of the working men—it is very good; but—take this to heart—remember that it is inconsistent with Free Trade. You cannot have Free Trade in goods in the sense in which our opponents use the word, and at the same time have protection of labour.

What is the experience of the world? Take the United States of America: take our own Colonies. It is universally admitted that in those countries the general standard of living, the position of comfort and prosperity in which the working classes exist, is superior to their condition in this country. They have a tariff. . . . You will not find, I believe, a single man of influence or importance, whether among the manufacturing classes or amongst the working men of America and the colonies, who will not tell you that the principle of the tariff is part of a system for the elevation of the working classes, and that if they adopted our policy of Free Imports it would absolutely be impossible for them to maintain the high level of general prosperity to which they have attained. . . .

If you determine to continue the policy of unrestricted imports in this country without reference to how they are produced, then in that case you cannot maintain any form of protection of labour. The competition of these cheaper goods, goods made cheaper by artificial causes, or by differences—natural differences some of them—between ourselves and the foreign countries concerned, will force down the prices, and you will have to take lower wages or lose your employment. This consideration of the necessity of meeting somehow the increased cost which may be produced by the higher standard of living touches the people of the East End more nearly, I think, than the population of any other part of the United Kingdom. . . .

But I am told, " you will increase the cost of living." Well, suppose I did; which is the better for a working man—to have a loaf a farthing dearer and plenty of money in his pocket, or to have a loaf for twopence or threepence and no money to buy it? . . . In my opinion the cost of living is not the most important thing for the working man to consider. What he has to consider as most important to him is the price which he gets for his labour. But, gentlemen, do not be deceived; it so happens that all that I want for the purposes of this crusade does not involve a farthing's increased cost of living to any working man. All that it requires is a scientific, a reasonable transposition of taxation. . . .

(b)

The whole question of the social condition of the poor is contained in this one word—employment. In the past this country was in an exceptional position. It was the workshop of the world. We were fortunate in agriculture, we were supreme in manufactures. That is no longer the case. We are richer than ever, but in totally different circumstances. Our competitors are gaining upon us in that which makes national greatness. We may be richer, and yet weaker. We may have more millionaires and fewer working men, and that is the direction in which we are tending. Now, while our competitors are excluding us from their markets, they are gaining greatly upon ours. We see the beginning, because it is only the beginning. Are you so foolish that you are going to wait until it is too late to find a remedy? . . . If you do not attend to these indications, if you are led astray, if you allow your party feelings to close your ears against the warnings which are given you in no party sense, then I say you will awake some day to find the source of your strength undermined, because you have mistaken a musty dogma of old-fashioned schools for the principle of your progress and of your national life. You have it still in your power, by your decision, to maintain the position of your country in the world. You may secure it if you will meet your children everywhere with open arms; if, at the same time, you will sharpen your weapons against those who are inclined to treat you badly; if you will hold your own against those who turn their back on you; if you will welcome those who are only anxious to co-operate with you in a greater future than any past that we have known. And then indeed you may hope to transmit to your descendants untarnished in lustre, undiminished in power, the sceptre of our Imperial dominion.

THE SOURCES,
AND SOME SUGGESTIONS FOR FURTHER READING

1. CONSERVATIVE DOCTRINE, as it was made.
BURKE'S *Works*, World Classics Edition: especially *Reflections on the Revolution in France*.

COLERIDGE:

The Friend, 1809–10 (Bohn's Standard Library).
Lay Sermons, 1816 and 1817.
On the Constitution of the Church and State (1830).
Essays on His Own Times, ed. by his Daughter, 1850.
Two Addresses on Sir Robert Peel's Bill (1818), ed. by Sir Edmund Gosse. Privately printed, 1913: also printed in Lucy Seton-Watson's *Coleridge at Highgate*.
The Political Thought of S. T. Coleridge, a Selection, by R. J. White. London, 1938.

PEEL:

An Address to the Electors of the Borough of Tamworth. London, 1834.
The Opinions of the Rt. Hon. Sir Robert Peel expressed in Parliament and in Public, ed. by W. T. Haly. London, 1843 (and 1850).

DISRAELI:

The Spirit of Whiggism, 1834.
The Vindication of the British Constitution, 1835.
The Runnymede Letters, 1836.
Sybil, 1845.
The Radical Tory, by H. W. J. Edwards. London, 1937. (Selections from Disraeli's writings and speeches.)

R. CHURCHILL:

Speeches of Lord Randolph Churchill, 1880–8, with notes, etc., by Louis J. Jennings, 2 vols. London, 1889.

J. CHAMBERLAIN:

Speeches of Rt. Hon. Joseph Chamberlain, ed. by Charles W. Boyd, with an Introduction by Rt. Hon. Austen Chamberlain, 2 vols. London, 1914.

2. LIVES OF CONSERVATIVE STATESMEN, containing documents

PEEL:

C. S. Parker: *Sir Robert Peel*, 1899.

Lord Mahon and E. Cardwell: *Memoirs of Sir Robert Peel*, 2 vols. London, 1856.

DISRAELI:

Life of Disraeli, by W. F. Monypenny and G. E. Buckle, 6 vols. London, 1910–20 (2 vol. ed. 1929).

SALISBURY:

Life of Robert, Marquis of Salisbury, by Lady Gwendolin Cecil. London, 1921.

R. CHURCHILL:

Lord Randolph Churchill, by Winston Spencer Churchill, 2 vols. London, 1906.

J. CHAMBERLAIN:

Life of Joseph Chamberlain, by J. L. Garvin, Vols. 1–3. London, 1932–4.

3. ANTHOLOGIES

The Political Thought of S. T. Coleridge; a Selection, edited with an Introduction by R. J. White. London, 1938.

The Radical Tory; Disraeli's political development, illustrated from his original writings and speeches, selected, edited and introduced by H. W. J. Edwards. London, 1937.

The Opinions of Sir Robert Peel, ed. by W. T. Haly. London, 1843 and 1850.

Anthology of British Historical Speeches and Orations, compiled by Ernest Rhys. Everyman Library, 714.

Selected Speeches on the Constitution, ed. by Cecil S. Emden, 2 vols. World's Classics, O.U.P., 1939.

Opinions and Arguments, A. J. Balfour. London, 1927.

4. TORIES AT TIMES, OR OF SORTS

COBBETT:

Autobiography of William Cobbett, or the *Progress of a Ploughboy to a Seat in Parliament*, ed. by William Reitzel. The Faber Library, No. 26, first published 1933.

RICHARD OASTLER:

Tory Radical; the life of Richard Oastler, by Cecil Driver. New York and O.U.P., 1946.

GLADSTONE:

The State in its relations with the Church. London, 1838.

CARLYLE:

Past and Present. London, 1843.

SHAFTESBURY:

Life and work of the 7th Earl of Shaftesbury, K.G., by Ernest Hodder, 3 vols. London, 1886.
Lord Shaftesbury, by J. L. and B. Hammond. London, 1923.

LORD JOHN MANNERS:

Lord John Manners and his friends, by Charles Whibley, 2 vols. Edinburgh, 1925.

T. S. ELLIOT:

The Idea of a Christian Society. London, 1939.

5. BOOKS ABOUT CONSERVATISM, PAST, PRESENT AND FUTURE

Conservatism, by Lord Hugh Cecil. Home University Library, 1912.
The Tory Tradition, by Sir Geoffrey Butler. London, 1914.
Conservatism and the Future, by Lord Eustace Percy, W. S. Morrison, etc. London, 1935.
Principles and Prejudices, by Kenneth Pickthorn. Signpost Books, 1943.
Ourselves, by G. M. Young. Signpost Books, 1944.
The Case for Conservatism, by Quintin Hogg. Penguin Books, 1947.

INDEX OF PROPER NAMES